The
Chihuahua
Handbook

D. Caroline Coile, Ph.D.

BARRON'S

Acknowledgments

The author is grateful to the members of the Chi Elite for so generously sharing their wealth of knowledge.

A Word About Pronouns

Many dog lovers feel that the pronoun "it" is not appropriate when referring to a pet that can be such a wonderful part of our lives. For this reason the Chihuahua in this book is referred to as "he" unless the topic specifically relates to female dogs. This by no means implies any preference, nor should it be taken as an indication that either sex is particularly problematic.

About the Author

D. Caroline Coile has written 32 books and hundreds of articles about dogs for both the scientific and lay press. Among her books are *Chihuahuas: A Complete Pet Owner's Manual, Barron's Encyclopedia of Dog Breeds*, and *Show Me! A Dog Showing Primer*. Among her dog writing awards are the Denlinger, Maxwell, Canine Health Foundation, and Eukanuba Canine Health awards. She holds a doctorate in the field of neuroscience and behavior, with special interests in canine sensory systems, genetics, and behavior.

Cover Credits

Paulette Johnson: bottom, left front cover and spine. All other cover photos are from Shutterstock.

Photo Credits

Carol Beuchat: page 135; Tara Darling: pages 19, 24, 38, 61, 66, 75, 77, 78, 86, 88, 99, 125, 126, 129, 133, 149, 157, 160, 163; Cheryl A. Ertelt: pages 6, 7, 54, 57, 95, 103, 136, 139, 140, 165; Jean Fogle: pages 12, 13, 15, 17, 22, 28, 30, 32, 41, 42, 43, 49, 51, 53, 58, 67, 80, 91, 122, 148, 151, 154; Isabelle Francais: pages 1, 4, 8, 44, 47, 63, 64, 72, 73, 93, 94, 110, 117, 118, 121, 132, 156, 158; Pets by Paulette: pages vi, vii, viii, 2, 11, 26, 29, 62, 65, 70, 71, 79, 83, 84, 111, 115, 130, 134, 143, 145, 146, 153.

All inquiries should be addressed to:
Barron's Educational Series, Inc.
250 Wireless Boulevard
Hauppauge, New York 11788
www.barronseduc.com

ISBN-13: 978-0-7641-4330-4
ISBN-10: 0-7641-4330-1

Library of Congress Catalog Card No. 2009031372

Library of Congress Cataloging-in-Publication Data
Coile, D. Caroline.
   The Chihuahua handbook / D. Caroline Coile. — 2nd ed.
      p. cm.
   Includes index.
   ISBN-13: 978-0-7641-4330-4
   ISBN-10: 0-7641-4330-1
   1. Chihuahua (Dog breed) I. Title.
   SF429.C45C64 2010
   636.76—dc22   2009031372

Printed in China
9 8 7 6 5 4 3

Important Note

This handbook tells the reader how to buy or adopt and care for a Chihuahua. The author and the publisher consider it important to point out that the advice given in the book is meant primarily for normally developed dogs of excellent physical health and good character.

Anyone who adopts a fully grown dog should be aware that the animal has already formed his basic impressions of human beings. The new owner should watch the animal carefully, including his behavior toward humans, and should meet the previous owner.

If the dog comes from a shelter, it may be possible to get some information on the dog's background and peculiarities there. There are dogs that, as a result of bad experiences with humans, behave in an unnatural manner or may even bite. Only people that have experience with dogs should take in such animals.

Caution is further advised in the association of children with dogs, in meeting with other dogs, and in exercising the dog without a leash.

Even well-behaved and carefully supervised dogs sometimes do damage to someone else's property or cause accidents. It is therefore in the owner's interest to be adequately insured against such eventualities, and we strongly urge all dog owners to purchase a liability policy that covers their dog.

Contents

Preface

Chihuahuas are among the most recognizable, yet least understood, of all dog breeds. They are more than just tiny dogs. They have a unique blend of personality characteristics that make sharing your life with one a constant mission of discovery. And once you feel you've grown to know one Chihuahua, you learn that the next one is totally different. Besides that, Chihuahuas have unique physical conditions that would be considered totally abnormal in other breeds, conditions that have even caught some non-Chihuahua-savvy veterinarians off guard.

Despite the intricacies involved in knowing and caring for Chihuahuas, they are attracting more and more people to their family. Chihuahua lovers come from all walks of life, but they tend to have one thing in common: they are unusually committed to their dogs and to providing the ultimate care for them.

That's why this book was written. *The Chihuahua Handbook* was developed for the Chihuahua owner who needs a little more advanced information about living with this unique breed. This book assumes you have some basic knowledge about dog care. If you need beginner informa-

tion, you are also urged to consult my more introductory book *Chihuahuas: A Complete Pet Owner's Manual.*

As you read, take note of some of the special sections. "Small Talk" sidebars add a morsel of extra, often little known, information to a section. "Small Wonder" sidebars introduce some exceptional and record-setting Chihuahuas. "Ay, Chihuahua!" sidebars provide in-depth information that may take a little extra thought to digest.

The Chihuahua Handbook was written to prepare the Chihuahua owner who wants to excel at Chihuahua ownership. After all, Chihuahuas already excel at people ownership.

Chapter One
Small Wonders

They say the eyes are the windows to the soul. Maybe that's why Chihuahuas have big, lustrous eyes that draw you into their spell; wide-open eyes that bare their souls to those they love. Yet, the Chihuahua holds a secret. The breed's past is cloaked in mystery; those few clues we do have are dark and shadowy. If you look deep enough into a Chihuahua's eyes, though, one thing is clear: if the eyes are the windows to the soul, then the Chihuahua has the biggest soul in all of dogdom.

A History Shrouded in Mystery

In the middle of the nineteenth century, American visitors to Mexico found a most unusual souvenir to take home: tiny dogs unlike any they had ever seen. Not only were these dogs unusually small, but they had some peculiar traits, such as a soft spot in their heads and flattened tails. The Americans named the little dogs according to the region of the border in which they were found, such as Arizona Dogs, Texas Dogs, or simply Mexican Dogs. However, so many

came from the Mexican state of Chihuahua that the name Chihuahua dogs (sometimes Chihuahua terriers) stuck. Dog shows were all the rage in Europe at the time; by the late 1800s interest in showing unusual purebred dogs had gained a strong foothold in the northeastern United States. James Watson was among the foremost dog authorities of his day, so when he reported about the tiny dogs he had acquired in Mexico, other dog fanciers took note.

We don't know much about these founding Chihuahuas. They varied widely in appearance, differing in size, refinement, and even coat. We know even less about how they got to where they were found. The tales about how these dogs came to inhabit such a desolate region varied as widely as the dogs themselves.

Made in Mexico

The most popular tale contends the Chihuahua is a native of Mexico. Many North- and Central-American cultures included domestic dogs as part of their diet for centuries. The Toltecs of Mexico described a small, plump, thick-necked dog with short, erect ears and tail that was bred for

**Small Talk
What's in a Name?**
In Mexico, the breed is known as the Chihuahueno.

Ay, Chihuahua!
In 2007, scientists discovered the gene mutation partially responsible for small size in dogs. This mutation suppresses the activity of the gene that codes for the hormone insulin-like growth factor 1 (IGF-1). Because the mutation is so widespread among dogs, it's believed to have originated very early in the history of domestic dogs.

food, primarily as a delicacy. Toltec carvings from the ninth century A.D. show a small dog with an uncanny resemblance to the Chihuahua, complete with a round head and erect ears. This dog was known as the Techichi and is thought to be the ancestor of many of the Central-American breeds.

When the Aztecs conquered the Toltecs, they adopted the Techichi as their own. The Techichi became an important animal in Aztec culture and religion. They were believed to have mystical powers, able to see into the future and to cure disease by transferring sickness to themselves or other people. A small red dog was believed to guide the souls of the dead to their underworld, helping them to cross the river that separated the world of the living from the world of the dead. Such a dog was kept as a valued member of every household, ready to guide the souls of any member of the family who should die. Of course, the dog had to be killed and placed into the grave with the person so he could also get to the underworld. Techichis, sometimes painted with vermilion, have been found in human graves all over Mexico. Some evidence exists that graves may have also included a dog so that the deceased could have a meal when they arrived in the underworld. Occasionally, a pottery figure of a dog was substituted for a real dog. In some areas, the dog would be burned along with the deceased in the belief that this process would transfer the person's sins to the dog.

Techichis were also sacrificed on a grander scale to appease the gods. Human sacrifices were an integral part of Aztec culture, and they often lived pampered lives until their date with destiny. The Techichis (preferably red or gray ones) earmarked for sacrifice lived in the temples of the priests and were probably also treated quite well until they were sent to meet the gods. No malice was held toward the dogs; sacrifice was an honored role.

Comprehending exactly how the Aztecs viewed these dogs is difficult. Some accounts suggest they lived as

Small Talk
The First Therapy Dogs
Small dogs have been used as living hot-water bottles throughout the world for centuries. Placing a warm dog onto an aching body part can be soothing, and it may be where the idea arose that the pain was being transferred from the person to the dog. Some historians speculate that this might be the basis for the idea that sins could be transferred from people to dogs by burning them together.

valued companions. If so, the Aztec's view of the afterlife no doubt enabled them to send the dogs on to the next world with far less a sense of loss than would be felt today.

The Spanish Conquest: When the Spaniards conquered the Aztecs in the 1500s, the Spaniards paid scant attention to the Aztecs' little dogs. Although a few were said to have been taken back to Europe, most were apparently abandoned. Their fate after that is unclear. Many people believe they became feral and existed off of birds and small rodents. This is somewhat less far-fetched than it

Small Talk
Prairie Dogs
One of the most fanciful tales regarding the Chihuahua is that the feral Techichi bred with prairie dogs, resulting in a small dog with a round head and flat tail that came to be known as the Chihuahua. This is genetically impossible, of course.

seems initially since the Techichi often had long hair and was not quite as small as the Chihuahua as we know it. Nonetheless, it does take a leap of faith to believe that these little dogs lived on their own for over three hundred years before emerging as the progenitor of the Chihuahua.

Made in Europe

Another theory of the Chihuahua's development contends that the breed is of European descent. Small lapdogs have been known to exist in Europe since ancient times. The Maltese is among the most ancient of all breeds, specifically mentioned in writings as early as 300 B.C. and brought to England by at least the fourteenth century. By the Middle Ages, miniaturized Greyhounds could be found throughout southern Europe. Dwarf Spaniels and Papillons were popular in sixteenth century

Spain, Italy, and France. These breeds demonstrate the remarkable variety of European toy dogs available to the Spaniards at the time they came to the Americas.

Unidentified dogs in art lend further credibility to the theory that the Chihuahua's progenitors may have come from Europe. The most well-known example is Botticelli's 1482 depiction of the life of Moses, which includes a small, smooth, Chihuahua-like dog with large eyes and ears.

A troubling aspect of this theory, however, is that if such a tiny and remarkable dog existed in Europe, why was he not remarked upon? True, he would not have been referred to as a Chihuahua. However, some record of him would seem likely. The Europeans were generally very good about recording the breeds and types of dogs that shared their lives. And with the European interest in breeding small lapdogs, why was the breed not nurtured and developed there? If an ancestor of the Chihuahua was present in sixteenth-century Europe, clearly it was not yet the same breed that was discovered in Mexico in the 1800s.

Made in Asia

Yet another theory names Asia as the Chihuahua's birthplace. The Far East was known as an early center of concerted efforts to produce miniature plants and animals and the greatest early successes there occurred with dogs. The Far East region counts among its creations two of the most ancient of all breeds, the Japanese Chin and the Pekingese. By the thirteenth century, they were joined by the Chinese Crested. But it's a long way from Asia to Central America.

Some people have speculated that the Asians brought little dogs with them to the Americas when they crossed the land bridge of the Bering Strait around 25,000 B.C. However, it seems unlikely that small dogs had been perfected at that very early date. If they were, it seems equally unlikely that they would be taken on great migrations. Another theory is that explorers from China's Chin Dynasty sailed across the ocean and settled in western Mexico around 400 B.C. Even if this were the case, it seems somewhat unlikely that these ancient mariners would choose to bring a colony of small dogs on their journey.

One bit of evidence that lends credence to the Asian theory is that Mexico, like Asia, is home to dogs that have a gene that causes hairlessness, a gene that does not seem to be found in dogs in other parts of the world. The Chinese Crested shares this same genetic oddity with the Mexican Hairless or Xoloitzcuintle. Some early reports of the Mexican dogs considered short-haired, long-haired, and hairless dogs to all be Chihuahuas. Only later were they divided into different varieties and breeds. Yet genetic mutations can occur, and it's not improbable that the same mutation could have occurred and been nurtured on the two continents completely independently of one another.

A Melting Pot

Perhaps the truth lies somewhere in a combination of theories. The Techichi was undoubtedly present in Mexico when Hernando de Soto and the Spanish Conquistadors arrived in the sixteenth century. It seems possible that the Spanish eventually brought some of the European lapdogs. One theory proposes that the Techichi was interbred with the Papillon and these dogs gave rise to the Chihuahua. Some dogs from Asian descent may have also arrived by way of the Spaniards. Still, any of these theories leaves a gap of three hundred years between the arrival of the Conquistadors and the discovery

**Small Talk
AKC Registered**
The first Chihuahua registered with the American Kennel Club (AKC) was appropriately named Midget. The year was 1904, and four more Chihuahuas were also registered that year. Eleven were entered in shows (registration was not a prerequisite for showing at the time). In contrast, 42,013 Chihuahuas were AKC registered in 1999 alone.

of the little dogs in Mexico. This gap will forever remain a mystery; perhaps the Chihuahua should keep some secrets.

The Chihuahua in the United States

Even after the Chihuahua was discovered and brought to the United States, its history is murky. Any small dog found near the border was probably labeled a Chihuahua, and these dogs were probably interbred with little regard for their finer points of conformation. The foremost breeding criterion was small size. How small a domestic dog can become has physical limits, however, and at some point, health often begins to suffer. In addition, by selecting on only the basis of size, other valuable traits of breed type were being lost in the shuffle. The resulting dogs tended to be very fragile and of varying types.

Once again, stories differ about what happened next.

Some stories contend that to combat the fragile dogs that dominated the breed, crosses to small terriers were made. These, however, resulted in long-legged, narrow-headed dogs (a trait that still emerges in the breed today). Others contend that no such crosses were made and that the variability and eventual progress were due to the variation already present in the gene pool.

The origin of the two coat varieties is also disputed. Some stories report that the first Chihuahuas were, in fact, longhaired. Evidence does point to the probability that the Techichi had a moderately long (if sparse) coat. Other stories claim that the long-coated variety resulted from crosses to the Papillon, Pomeranian, or Yorkshire Terrier after the breed came to the notice of American fanciers.

Small Wonder
The first AKC Champion Chihuahua was Ch Beppie, a female born in 1903.

Once again, the truth very likely lies in a combination of these stories. Some early reports stated that both smooth-coated and long-coated dogs were found along the border, so both types could have been present in those early dogs. In the early 1900s, purity of pedigree was not a priority in creating a winning show dog or successful breeding animal. Registration requirements were quite loose. They often required only that a dog look like a particular breed. Judicious crosses to other breeds in order to introduce certain traits were acceptable and not at all unusual. After all, virtually every breed results from crosses between breeds or strains at some time in its history. If such crosses were made, perhaps Chihuahua fanciers should be grateful. After all, the Chihuahua as we know it is the result.

Entering the Mainstream

Despite their appeal, the Chihuahua's popularity grew slowly. Just as today, most Chihuahua owners were content simply to enjoy their dogs at home and weren't interested in promoting or exhibiting them. Nonetheless, by 1923 enough serious interest had developed that a group of fanciers formed the Chihuahua Club of America. By working together, they arrived at the first description of

Small Wonder

The first Chihuahua to be awarded Best in Show was Ch Attas' Gretchen, in 1951. Not until 1975 did a Long Coat win a Best in Show. The record-setting win was finally achieved by Ch Snow Bunny d'Casa de Cris.

the ideal Chihuahua, resulting in the first Chihuahua Standard of Excellence (see page 132 for the current version). They also held specialty shows spotlighting the Chihuahua. The first independent specialty show occurred in 1946.

Entries at shows were modest for many years. Long and Smooth Coats were exhibited against each other until 1952, when they were split into two varieties of the same breed. This split meant that although they could still be interbred, they would be shown separately and compete for Best of Variety rather than Best of Breed. The only time Best of Breed is awarded is at an independent specialty (one held not as part of an all-breed show).

As pivotal as the efforts of dedicated Chihuahua breeders were, they were not the only ones to promote the breed. One of the breed's greatest admirers probably popularized the breed more than any breeder. He was Xavier Cugat, known as the Rumba King. He made his Chihuahuas one of his trademarks, appearing with them first in movies and later in his weekly television show. With national exposure, the little dogs from south of the border caught and held the public's imagination. By 1964, the Chihuahua had rocketed to the third most popular breed in America—and it's never strayed too far from that position since.

Curse of the Chihuahua

Somewhere between the threat of extinction and that of exploitation lies a comfortable state of moderate popularity—a state the Chihuahua has not enjoyed for a long time. The Chihuahua's curse is its appeal.

The Chihuahua has been among the most recognizable and popular of breeds in the United States—indeed, around the world—for many years. With popularity comes many burdens. Not everybody who is drawn to a popular breed has the right motives or background. Some are drawn to it not because they love the breed, but because they want to profit from it. As the Chihuahua breed shot up in popularity, individual Chihuahuas paid a heavy price. Cage upon cage of Chihuahuas lived out their lives as puppy-producing machines, providing adorable Chihuahua puppies for an eager but unsuspecting public. Too many families, understandably smitten with their dear pets, also chose to breed them. The result was a mushrooming population explosion.

At some point, the number of people who were truly suited to share their lives with a Chihuahua was surpassed by the number of Chihuahuas available. It takes a special match of person and dog to make a successful life together with any breed of dog, much less one with the unique traits of a Chihuahua. And, as supply exceeded demand, prices fell and more unsuitable people bought a Chihuahua on a whim. It was only a matter of time before this once rare and cherished breed was found peering from the cages at animal shelters.

Through it all, a core of dedicated breeders remained. Although sur-

rounded by others who were profiting from their beloved breed, they instead chose to sacrifice and breed with quality as their prime directive. They challenged their dogs against the breed standard and challenged themselves to find even better representatives with each generation. They checked their dogs for health problems and chose not to perpetuate those problems that could detract from a long and happy life.

Despite their long-lived popularity, the Chihuahua has fared extremely well. Other breeds that have found themselves in the same situation have not been so lucky. When people breed for profit or out of naïveté, they too often spread hereditary diseases through a breed. The Chihuahua has remarkably few hereditary diseases, though. Perhaps the Chihuahua's ancestors did fend for themselves in the wilds of the Mexican desert, culling out the less fit and imbuing the offspring with a healthy gene pool. And no doubt Chihuahuas' amiable and adaptive personalities have allowed them to win over and train even those people who may not really have been Chihuahua material when they first met.

Few breeds of dogs can claim the almost fanatic dedication that Chihuahua owners feel toward their dogs. These dogs bond so closely with their special people that it is as though they cast a spell over them. Perhaps the Aztecs were right when they attributed magic powers to their little dogs.

Chapter Two
Precious Little Choices

Taking care of a Chihuahua takes time, energy, money, and commitment. For that investment, you will get back very few tangible rewards. Luckily, the intangible rewards prove that you *can* buy love . . . just make sure you get the best love money can buy.

Sizing Up the Chihuahua

Chihuahuas are in a class by themselves in the canine world, and it's not simply because they're the world's smallest dog.

Temperament: Chihuahuas are loyal beyond belief and tend to choose one person as their special companion. These traits are great if you want a special friend always by your side or in your lap. They might not be great if you expect your dog to warm up to a constant parade of strangers or be on his own a good deal of the day. Chihuahuas are intelligent, quick-witted, and very capable of manipulating you to do their bidding. Watching them in action as they figure out how to get you to bend to

their will is part of the enchantment of living with a Chihuahua, but if you absolutely never can say "*No,*" you may find yourself at the mercy of a little Napoleon. Chihuahuas are incredibly brave for their size—but they are very small. This means that at times their bravado gets them into more trouble than they can handle. At times they do realize how vulnerable they are, however, and unless socialized from an early age, they may be overwhelmed by crowds and events.

Size Matters: From a practical point of view, the Chihuahua's small size is generally an asset. Small dogs are easier to feed, groom, transport, and clean up after. Yet this small size still comes at some cost. Small dogs are susceptible to injury from accidents that large dogs might not even notice. Their size makes them vulnerable to injuries from other dogs, careless adults, and rough children. Although they are excellent watchdogs and may try to be good protection dogs, a Chihuahua will be unlikely to hold off any but the most cowardly mugger. Nor would a Chihuahua be a good candidate for a marathon jogging partner. The Chi-

huahua's small body makes retaining body heat more difficult, and they cannot tolerate cold temperatures. Of course, that makes them all the more eager to snuggle up in your lap. It's no secret that Chihuahuas pack more love to the pound than any other breed of dog. Great dogs really do come in small packages.

Coat Type: One of your first decisions is whether you want a Long or Smooth Coat. This is mostly a matter of preference. Some people contend the Long Coats are a little calmer, but others disagree. The long coat is not so thick that it needs a lot of extra grooming, but it does need a little more care. An experienced breeder should be able to tell a Long Coat from a Short Coat by the age of three or four weeks. One telltale sign is a suggestion of a ridge down the back line. Don't expect a long coat to develop fully until a year or more of age.

By the Numbers: Chihuahuas are addictive. Their small size makes adding more and more to your household very tempting. After all, they don't eat much and don't take up much room. But don't lose sight of the fact that each Chihuahua needs as much, if not more, love and attention than a large breed of dog. At some point, you may surpass your ability to love each dog adequately. Also consider that veterinary bills are not appreciably cheaper for small dogs, so each dog you add will be adding a financial responsibility as well.

Chihuahuas are noted for being clannish, preferring the company of other Chihuahuas to that of other breeds. They will lower themselves, however, to consort with other breeds, especially if they are raised with them so the Chihuahuas come to accept the other breeds as honorary Chihuahuas. No matter how close the relationship, certain precautions should be taken when Chihuahuas share a home with larger dogs. Dogs can play roughly or even snap unpredictably over food or a toy—actions that might have dire consequences for a Chihuahua.

A Lick and a Promise: So there you have it: the good, the bad, and the snugly. Before you decide a Chihuahua is for you, make sure you're good enough for a Chihuahua. Chihuahuas become so attached to their human families that if you later decide you've changed your mind, you will be breaking a little dog's heart. Even worse, however, is to find you don't have the time, love, or available lap space to satisfy your Chihuahua's needs. Chihuahuas are so small that they are almost too easy to stick into a corner and ignore. Fortunately, most Chihuahuas will not tolerate such behavior on your part! These tiny dogs have huge hearts, and they, in turn, are huge responsibilities.

Looking for Love

That something so little can have such a huge effect on your life is hard to believe. However, once you invite a Chihuahua into your lap, your life will never be the same. You will sacrifice much for your little dog but get even more in return. You will increase your chances of getting the very best love money can buy if you choose

> **Small Talk**
> **Good Breeders**
> • Are familiar with and screen for Chihuahua health concerns.
> • Can compare their dogs with the breed standard feature by feature.
> • Have photos and pedigrees of both parents and other relatives.
> • Breed sparingly and dedicate their breeding efforts to only one or two breeds.
> • Belong to a local or national Chihuahua club.
> • Are involved in some sort of Chihuahua competition.
> • Ask you lots of questions about your facilities, family, lifestyle, your past history with dogs, and expectations for your new dog.
> • Require that should you ever have to relinquish the dog, they get first refusal.
> • Provide a medical history, pedigree, registration information, and written care instructions with each puppy.
> • Usually do not allow puppies to leave them until they are at least 12 weeks of age and even older for smaller pups. Some breeders prefer to keep their Chihuahuas until 16 weeks of age.

your source, and your Chihuahua, wisely. To do that, you need to know how to tell good breeders from bad breeders and good Chihuahuas from great Chihuahuas.

Sources: Most people seeking a new Chihuahua don't want a show dog, just a new best friend. Their most common sources are newspaper ads, friends, pet stores, hobby breeders, and rescue. Of these, hobby breeders and rescue organizations should be your first choices. Hobby breeders can be located through Chihuahua clubs, dog magazines (especially Chihuahua magazines), or kennel pages on the Internet. As in all walks of life, some breeders are more ethical and knowledgeable than others. Try to visit prospective breeders personally and see for yourself how the adults look and act and how puppies are being raised.

Hobby breeders have made producing superior Chihuahuas a main focus of their lives. They will have proven their dogs in some form of competition and screened them for hereditary health problems. Despite these breeder's best efforts, not every pup will turn out to be competition quality. These pet- (or companion-) quality pups will still have profited from the breeders' knowledge of genetics and puppy care, and will still need good homes. Good hobby breeders will screen prospective pet homes no less diligently than their other prospective homes. They will expect you to keep them abreast of your pup's progress and come to them with any problems, just like all of their puppy buyers.

Dog Shows: A good place to find serious breeders is at a dog show or especially, a Chihuahua specialty show (a prestigious show in which only Chihuahuas compete). The annual Chihuahua Club of America National Specialty attracts hundreds of competitors from around the country. Not only can you meet more good breeders at large specialties, but you can also get a better idea of the particular type of Chihuahua you

prefer and what traits are most important to you.

If you have your heart set on a show-quality Chihuahua, try to attend several specialty shows before deciding on a breeder. Your best breeder is one who produces healthy dogs with excellent temperaments that also conform to the AKC Chihuahua standard. The breeder should have a record of producing a high percentage of such dogs. Producing winners is not difficult if you breed enough puppies. The challenge is in doing so ethically, breeding with restraint and taking responsibility for every puppy throughout his life.

Get a Life!
Chihuahua Rescue

Sometimes we don't pick our new family members; they pick us. They may insert themselves into our lives when we least expect it. They may present themselves when we were looking for quite a different dog. They may burrow into our hearts when we said we had no more room. Somehow they stay when we vowed they were just visiting—and we never know how we got along without them.

The rising popularity of the Chihuahua has resulted in an overabundance of adult Chihuahuas that have been given up by their first families. Some are advertised in the newspaper, some are forfeited to animal shelters, and some are fostered by Chihuahua rescue organizations.

These Chihuahuas come in all descriptions and have varied histories. However, the typical rescue Chihuahua is a young adult whose human family found out they underestimated the commitment that even a tiny dog entailed.

Before adopting a rescue dog, find out as much as you can about his background; the reason he was given up; how he relates to men, women, children, and other pets; and any temperament or health problems he may have. You may feel guilty looking at a dog in need with a critical eye. However, you are doing that dog no favor at all if you can't cope with him any better than his former owners could. To give a Chihuahua in need a place in your home and heart, contact a Chihuahua rescue group (page 164).

You might also consider volunteering as a foster home, providing a temporary haven for a homeless Chihuahua awaiting a forever home. But be forewarned: more often than not, temporary homes end up being permanent!

Not all adults come from needy circumstances. Breeders may have an adult dog, often retired from the showring, available that would relish the chance to live as a pampered pet. Whatever the source, consider adopting an adult in need of a family. They have years of love to share.

To Good Health

No matter what your plans are for your Chihuahua, good health is a prerequisite. The Chihuahua, like every breed of dog, has its own special set of health concerns. Many of the problems to which it is somewhat predisposed have a hereditary basis. You may be able to avoid them to some extent by choosing your Chihuahua carefully. Even the most carefully bred Chihuahua is not immune from the threat of hereditary health problems, but take heart: most Chihuahuas live long lives free of any serious hereditary problems. The most prevalent hereditary (or possibly hereditary) conditions in Chihuahuas are patellar luxation, hydrocephalus, tracheal collapse, and (in puppies) hypoglycemia.

• Patellar luxation occurs when the dog's kneecap slips out of place, causing the dog to hold his leg up and hop for a few steps. Depending on the severity, the kneecap may or may not pop back into place. This is a painful condition that often requires surgery. The Orthopedic Foundation for Animals (OFA) maintains a database of the results from patellar examinations of Chihuahuas. However, many breeders prefer to have their dogs checked and certified by their own veterinarian without going to the additional small expense of OFA registration. Because of the strong hereditary component of this problem, you should obtain your puppy from parents who have both been cleared of this problem through the OFA or who have both a certificate of the same from a local veterinarian. Your chances of getting a Chihuahua with healthy knees are even better if the family on both sides, including brothers and sisters, grandparents and great-grandparents, are certified clear. For more information about patellar luxation, see pages 100–101.

• Hydrocephalus occurs when fluid builds up within parts of the brain. Because the skull cannot expand, the high pressure interferes with normal blood circulation, and the brain can be damaged. Treatment is difficult, and dogs may be slightly mentally slow for life. Hydrocephalus occurs more often in certain small breeds, including Chihuahuas. The genetic component, if any, is unclear. Until more is known, current recommendations are to avoid breeding affected dogs and, as much as possible, to avoid breeding dogs with affected relatives. For more information, see pages 101–102.

• Tracheal collapse occurs in some middle-aged or older Chihuahuas when the cartilage making up the rings of the trachea weakens. This causes the airway to become obstructed and results in reflexive coughing. The condition tends to get worse with time. Chihuahuas are among the breeds most often affected; however, the hereditary component, if any, is not clear. For more information, see pages 90–91, 93.

• Hypoglycemia occurs when blood sugar levels fall dangerously low. It is more likely to happen in young

puppies of small breeds, especially when stressed or when feeding is delayed. The condition is not considered hereditary. Rather, it is simply a consequence of an immature liver and a small body. The best way to avoid hypoglycemia is to get an older puppy or to be very careful that your pup does not get stressed or hungry. For more information, see pages 127–129.

• Other conditions to which Chihuahuas are more susceptible compared with other breeds are discussed on pages 93–105.

The Molera

The molera, or open fontanel, is a common trait in many well-bred and healthy Chihuahuas. It can be felt as a soft spot of various sizes on the top of the dog's head. It is actually where

The molera is an open space in the skull where the bones that normally fuse in most breeds remain open in many Chihuahuas.

the frontal and parietal bones of the cranium, which usually fuse soon after birth, remain unfused instead. In most Chihuahuas, the bones continue to fuse somewhat as the dog matures. By the age of one and one-half years, only about 16 percent of moleras are closed. Eventually about 50 percent close—although this may not occur until three years of age. Only a small percentage of moleras remain large.

So much has the molera been associated with the Chihuahua that in years past, the purity of a Chihuahua without a molera was suspect. More recently, the molera has been blamed for the occurrence of hydrocephalus in the breed. Many veterinarians, upon seeing a pup with a large molera, express their concern about the pup's future health. Fortunately, research has since demonstrated that a molera of any size does not predispose the Chihuahua to hydrocephalus. Veterinary neurologists have stated that the presence of a small molera is not a detriment to good health. Some argument can even be made that its presence allows the brain room for swelling that might occur subsequent to hydrocephalus or trauma. Nonetheless, the skull encases the dog's brain for a good reason—protection. Although the tissue covering the molera is tough, it cannot protect the brain from injury in the way the bones of the skull can. Chihuahuas with moleras should certainly be safeguarded from any blows to the head—but then, so should all Chihuahuas.

Tempest in a Teacup

Many people are drawn to the tiniest Chihuahuas available. Ads for so-called teacup or pocket-sized Chihuahuas often boast of such tiny dogs. As in any breed, some variation in size occurs between individuals. No separate class of tiny Chihuahua exists, however, and the Chihuahua Club of America frowns on the use of these misleading terms. Despite their undeniable appeal, several drawbacks accompany these dogs. Chihuahuas are already pushing the envelope as far as size and health are concerned. Choosing the tiniest of an already tiny breed tends to magnify the chance and severity of any possible health problems. Some breeders report a larger incidence of hypoglycemia, large moleras, hydrocephalus, tooth loss, and injuries in the tiny Chihuahuas. These puppies, especially, may not thrive as well as larger Chihuahua puppies. A tiny Chihuahua is not a good choice for an inexperienced dog owner. If your heart is set on a tiny Chihuahua, you might do best to wait until the pup is older before taking one home with you.

Remember, the Chihuahua standard gives no preference for smaller dogs within the 6-pound (2.7 kg) weight limit. Besides, is 6 pounds (2.7 kg) not tiny enough? Many breeders suggest a dog weighing about 4 pounds (1.8 kg) is ideal—small enough to be very cute yet large enough to be fairly sturdy. If you want to compete with your Chihuahua in obedience or agility, a dog that is near the top of the allowed weight limit will generally have an easier time. Even conformation dogs may be hindered by a tiny size. Since many shows are held outdoors with somewhat tall grass, the tiniest Chihuahuas will have difficulty moving with ease. If you intend your Chihuahua as a companion for a child, a larger dog is usually better suited. A rough guide to adult weight can be arrived at by doubling the pup's weight at 14 weeks of age. Of course this is not exact, but it can give you a general idea for most lines of Chihuahuas.

The Chihuahua of Your Choice

Even if you have no competitive goals, remember the essentials of any good Chihuahua: good health, good temperament, and good looks.

Health: For health, ask about the longevity, health, and health clearances of your potential pup's ancestors. The Chihuahua Club of America has determined that the essential tests for Chihuahua parents are heart, eye, and patellar clearances. Chihuahuas with certified results of all three tests can be listed in the Canine Health Information Center database (*www.caninehealthinfo.org*). This is a good place to look for breeders who are interested in health; you'll notice that many of the dog listings in the database start with the same kennel name. Don't discount a line with some problems since no line of dogs is perfect. Besides, some other breeders may simply not be as honest in disclosing problems. The major health clearance for Chihuahua is certification that the dog is free of patellar luxation.

If you want a male for conformation (or breeding), be sure both of his testicles have descended into the scrotum by the time you take him home. Although the testicles of some Chihuahuas descend very late, do not depend on it happening unless you don't mind falling in love with a pup you may not be able to show. Of course, these dogs can compete in obedience and agility, and they make great companions. No matter how much research you do into the background of any puppy, there is no guarantee that your dog will live a long and healthy life, but you can increase the odds by choosing a dog from a healthy family.

Temperament: For temperament, consider the essentials stated in the standard: "alert, with terrier-like qualities." Of course you also want a dog that is intelligent and loving. By eight weeks of age, Chihuahua puppies should be curious and investigative. A puppy that freezes in place or always heads home when carried a short distance away from his littermates may not have the self-confidence typical of the Chihuahua. It's human nature to go for the extremes in temperament, but for most family companions you're better off choosing the pup that is neither the boldest nor the shyest in the litter. Since the breeders have had more time to get to know the puppies' personalities, consider their opinion seriously. Many people who can't decide let the puppy pick them. It's hard to say no to a little tyke that bounces over to say hello and ends up nibbling your fingers and falling asleep in your lap. Of course, you may be in big trouble if you end up with a whole lap full!

Looks: For looks, again consider the essentials of the Chihuahua stan-

Small Talk
Puppy Checklist

Your prospective puppy should:
- Have his first vaccinations and deworming.
- Be outgoing and active. Avoid a puppy that shows signs of fearfulness or aggressiveness. If a pup is apathetic or sleepy, he may have just eaten, but it could also be a sign of sickness.
- Be clean, with no missing hair, crusted or reddened skin, or signs of parasites.
- Have no indication of redness or irritation around the anus.
- Have pink gums; pale gums may indicate anemia.
- Not be coughing, sneezing, or vomiting.
- Not be thin or potbellied.
- Have clean eyes, ears, and nostrils, free of any discharge.
- Not be dehydrated, which can suggest repeated vomiting or diarrhea. Test for dehydration by picking up a fold of skin and releasing it. The skin should pop back into place.
- Not have rear dewclaws. Some Chihuahuas are born with extra toes on the inside of the hind legs. Because these can be injured by getting caught on things, reputable breeders remove them at birth.

dard: "A graceful, alert, swift-moving little dog with saucy expression, compact . . . not to exceed 6 pounds (2.7 kg)." The Chihuahua is usually between 6 and 9 inches (15 and 23 cm) tall and slightly longer than its height at the withers. The head is an apple head, with full, but not protruding, eyes and large, erect ears. The ears may not be standing on a very

young Chihuahua or on one that is teething. When moving, the head is carried proudly and the tail is carried confidently.

Your criteria will be more stringent if your pup is destined for a show career. In this case, you should rely on the advice of the breeder, who will know better than anyone how dogs from that line mature. You may wish to purchase an older puppy or adult if you definitely want a show- or breeding-quality dog. Your personal preferences do count; consider coat type, color, and size, among other things.

You've done your best. You've studied the breed and know you are willing to take on the responsibility of a very special dog. You've searched for a reputable breeder, bypassing the newspaper ads and other easily accessible sources in favor of breeders who have dedicated their lives to producing healthy dogs representative of the best this breed has to offer. You've found the litter that comes closest to meeting your ideals and finally selected the pup of your dreams. Now make those dreams come true.

Chapter Three
It's a Small World

The Chihuahua has always expected to be a real member of the family, supervising family activities from the comfort of your lap and joining in family adventures. In turn, Chihuahua owners expect their charges to act civilized, not using the antique furniture as a chew stick or the heirloom rugs as a bathroom. True, your Chihuahua will soon have you rushing to satisfy his slightest whim, but try to at least maintain some pretense of being in charge!

Welcome Home

Your Chihuahua now faces the transition from canine litter member to human family member. Every day will be full of novel experiences and new rules. Your pup is naturally inquisitive and will need you to guide him toward becoming a well-mannered member of the household.

Half the excitement of welcoming a new dog is preparing for the big homecoming. Puppy proofing your home will be a lot easier if you do it before your new puppy is underfoot undoing everything as fast as you can do it. Much of the fun comes from a Chihuahua accessory buying spree. The best sources for supplies are large pet stores, dog shows, and discount pet catalogs.

Collaring Your Chihuahua

Choosing a collar for a tiny dog presents some special challenges. A collar that is too large can be very dangerous. Not only can it get hung on twigs or furniture, but most often, the dog's own lower jaw can get caught in it. The dog will panic, rake at his face (possibly injuring his eyes in the process), and can run into things in his frenzy. Several Chihuahuas have ultimately broken their jaws from such mishaps. Playmates can also get their jaws hung in collars; dogs of several breeds have been choked to death in such tragic circumstances. For this reason, some people prefer never to leave any collar on their Chihuahua unless they are with the dog. The downside of this is that if your Chihuahua were ever to get out, a collar with tags should help him be reunited with you. Don't hang every tag you can think of on your Chihuahua's collar, though; they're heavy! The ideal tag is one that does not hang at all but is secured flat on the collar. Consider a tattoo or microchip for permanent identification whether your dog wears tags or not.

Many people find cat collars work well with small Chihuahuas. Some of these have an elastic portion so the collar can be pulled off if the cat (or dog) gets it caught on something. Other people prefer a small, rolled leather collar. A choke collar is out of the question. You might as well send your dog out to play wearing a hangman's noose.

Walking your dog is another matter. When doing so, whatever collar you place onto your dog must not be able to come off. Too many Chihuahuas have become frightened and backed out of their collars and into danger. If you use a buckle collar, make sure it cannot slip over the dog's head no matter what happens. You can also either use a martingale collar, which is a leash and collar combination that tightens up to only a certain extent when the dog pulls, or use a harness. A harness has several advantages. Dogs cannot hurt their necks if they are wearing one, which is especially important in dogs that may be predisposed to tracheal collapse (see page 90). They cannot back out of one, and in an emergency, they can be lifted up in the air by a harness without hurting them. The disadvantage is that constant use of the harness may cause the elbows to spread away from the body, which would be very detrimental to a show dog's chances in the ring. A properly trained dog, who pulls against neither a harness or a collar, is the safest solution overall.

Chihuahua Quarters

Most Chihuahuas are lucky. They aren't tied to a chain in the yard or banned to a kennel run out back. Some are less fortunate; their owners seem to think they will be fine in the

Small Talk
Chihuahua Start-Up Kit

• Leash: nylon, web, or leather—never chain! An adjustable show lead is good for puppies.

• Lightweight retractable leash: better for older adults; be sure not to drop the leash since it can retract toward the pup and could frighten him.

• Stainless-steel food and water bowls: avoid plastic; it can cause allergic reactions and hold germs.

• Crate: large enough for an adult to stand up in without having to lower his head. You may need to divide it so that the available space for a puppy is smaller. See pages 24–26 for a description.

• Exercise pen: see page 27 for a description.

• Toys: latex squeakies, fleece-type toys, balls, stuffed animals, stuffed socks (stuffed with crackly sounding paper), or empty plastic soda jugs. Make sure no parts of toys, including squeakers or plastic eyes, can be pulled off and swallowed.

• Chew bones: the equivalent of a teething ring for babies.

• Antichew preparations, such as Bitter Apple: the unpleasant taste dissuades pups from chewing on items sprayed with it.

• Baby gate(s): for placing parts of your home off-limits. Do not use the accordion-style gates. A dog can get his head stuck in this gate and asphyxiate.

• Soft brush.

• Nail clippers: guillotine type is easier to use.

• Poop scoop: two-piece rake type is best for grass.

• Dog shampoo: see pages 71–72 for choices.

• First-aid kit: see page 107 for contents.

• Food: start with the same food the pup is currently eating.

---

garage or basement. They will not. Chihuahuas are people dogs, and they need to be in the house. This doesn't mean they need the run of the house, though. Certainly at first, they should not have the whole house in which to get into trouble. Before bringing your puppy home, you should decide what parts of your home will be off-limits.

The Crate: Many new dog owners are initially appalled at the idea of putting their pet into a crate as though he were some wild beast. At times, though, your Chihuahua pup can seem a wild beast, and a crate is one way to save your home from ruination and yourself from insanity. Perhaps more importantly, a crate can also provide a safe and quiet haven for your youngster. Just as you hope to find peace and security as you sink into your own bed at night, your pup needs a place that he can call his own, a place he can seek out whenever the need for rest and solitude arise. It's also a place you can put your pup where you know he will be out of harm's way when you have company or workers in the house. When used properly, your Chihuahua will come to think of the crate not as a way to keep himself in but as a way to keep others out!

Don't expect your dog to stay in a crate all day, every day, while you are at work. Overuse of the crate is not only unfair and even cruel to the dog, but it can also lead to behavioral problems. A Chihuahua is an intelligent, active dog. To lock one inside a crate without stimulation can result in such frustration and anxiety that the dog can begin to resent the crate and act uncontrollably when out of the crate. A crate should be the canine equivalent of a toddler's crib. It is a place for nap time, a place where you can leave your pup without worry of him hurting himself or your home. The crate is not a place for punishment, nor is it a storage box for your dog when you're through playing with him. Rethink getting a Chihuahua (or any dog) if you plan for him to live in a crate.

Small Talk
Chihuahuas on High
Chihuahuas love to survey their kingdom from a high perch and also won't be happy unless they are in your lap or with you on your bed. But how do they get there? Some jump. Many Chihuahuas have an amazing ability to jump several times their own height. Others could jump but far prefer for their personal servant (you) to lift them. Jumping down can be dangerous, though. A good rule of thumb is that if your dog can't jump up onto something by himself, he should not be allowed to jump off of that something. Teach your Chihuahua to stay until you lift him down. Many owners construct ramps or steps to favorite spots, such as the bed or sofa. These can be elaborate ramps with rails or simply a stack of pillows.

Nonetheless, the crate has its place in training. Place the crate into a corner of a quiet room but not too far from the rest of the family. Place the pup into the crate when he begins to fall asleep, and he will become accustomed to using the crate as his bed. Be sure to place a soft blanket on the bottom. By taking the pup directly from the crate to the outdoors upon awakening, the crate will be one of the handiest housebreaking aids at your disposal.

The X-Pen: An exercise pen (or X-pen) fulfills

many of the same functions as a crate. X-pens are transportable, wire, folding playpens for dogs, typically about 4 feet by 4 feet (1.2 m by 1.2 m). X-pens are a reasonable solution when you must be gone for a long time. The pup can relieve himself on paper or in a litter box in one corner, sleep on a soft bed in the other, and frolic with his toys all over! The X-pen is like having a little yard inside. It provides a safe time-out area when you just need some quiet time for yourself. If you use an X-pen, cover the floor beneath it with thick plastic (an old shower curtain works well), and then add towels or washable rugs for traction and absorbency. Again, do not expect to stick your Chihuahua into an X-pen all day every day and still have a sane dog.

Good Fences Make Live Chihuahuas

The number one Chihuahua accessory and lifesaver is a securely fenced yard. In today's world of automobiles and suburbs, a loose dog is at best an unwelcome visitor and, more often, a dead dog. A Chihuahua cannot roam the neighborhood and expect to live a long life. Make sure your fence is absolutely Chihuahua proof from the outset. A fence that can be dug under or squeezed through only teaches the dog to look even harder for vulnerable spots. A tiny dog loose in a big world won't get many second chances. For your

Small Talk
Sun Worshippers
One of a Chihuahua's favorite things in life is sunbathing. Make sure your Chihuahua's quarters have a patch of sunlight for your dog to soak up during the day. Of course, make sure he also has a way to get out of direct light when he's had enough! Note: a Chihuahua with a pink nose can be sunburned and even develop skin cancer. Pink-nosed dogs should wear sunscreen on their nose if they are in the sun for prolonged periods. The belly of any Chi can also become burned if he sunbathes on his back.

dog's safety and your own peace of mind, get a fence you never have to worry about. Invisible fences are not advisable for Chihuahuas. The collar they must wear is too heavy, the shock they receive from crossing the boundary too intense, and the protection a real fence affords Chihuahuas against neighborhood dogs and dognappers is absent with those fences.

Dangers also abound within the yard. Check for poisonous plants, bushes with sharp, broken branches at Chihuahua eye level, and trees with dead branches or heavy fruits or pine cones in danger of falling. If you have a pool, be aware that although Chihuahuas can swim, they cannot do so for long and can't get out of a pool without help. Even if the pool has steps, your Chihuahua won't know where to find them unless he has had lots of practice.

Although somewhat the exception, some Chihuahuas enjoy a brief swim. If you wish to encourage this behavior, get a shallow pool that your dog can splash around in, one not so deep that his feet can't touch the ground. Gradually increase the water depth, and get right in there with your dog. Help him swim at first by elevating his rear; this way, he won't be splashing on top of the water with his front paws. Always be there to supervise; most Chihuahuas can't swim for very long. In cool weather, you can use your bathtub. Swimming is an excellent exercise for dogs with arthritis or injured limbs. Of course, most Chihuahuas prefer just soaking up the rays poolside or sharing your float.

Safety Begins at Home

Your puppy will naturally want to explore every nook and cranny of your house. Any place your Chihuahua may wander must be Chihuahua proofed. Imagine if you had a baby that could run faster than you could, was small enough to crawl under all your furniture, had an irresistible urge to gnaw on everything in sight, yet was so small and fragile he could be hurt or even killed by a moment's carelessness. That describes a Chihuahua puppy.

For starters, watch out for these dangerous situations around the house.

• Puppies love to chew electric cords in half and even lick outlets. These activities can result in death from shock, severe burns, and loss of jaw and tongue tissue. Pups can also pull electric appliances down on themselves by pulling on cords.

• Jumping up onto an unstable object (such as a bookcase) could cause the object to come crashing down, perhaps crushing the puppy.

• Do not allow the puppy near the edges of high decks, balconies, or staircases. Use baby gates, temporary plastic fencing, or chicken wire if needed in dangerous areas.

• Doors can be a hidden danger area. Everyone in your family must be made to understand the danger of slamming a door. Use doorstops to ensure that the wind does not blow doors suddenly shut or that the

puppy does not go behind the door to play. Be especially cautious with swinging doors. A puppy may try to push one open, become caught, try to back out, and strangle. Clear glass doors may not be seen, and the puppy could be injured running into them. Never close a garage door with a puppy darting about. Finally, doors leading to unfenced outdoor areas should be kept securely shut. A closed screen door is a vital safety backup feature.

• Take precautions to prevent a Chihuahua with a molera (see page 18), especially a large one, from hitting his head in that area. Don't allow him to play under furniture where he could

Small Talk
The Dog Ate What?

Pica, the ingestion of nonfood items (such as wood, fabric, or soil), can be a problem is some dogs. Talk to your veterinarian about possible health problems that could contribute to these specific hungers and about possible problems that could result from eating these items.

The most common and disturbing nonfood item eaten by dogs is feces. This habit, called coprophagy, has been blamed on boredom, stress, hunger, poor nutrition, and excessively rich nutrition. However, none of these has proved a completely satisfactory explanation. Food additives are available that make the resulting stool less savory, and you can also try adding hot pepper to the stool, but a determined dog will not be deterred. The best cure is immediate removal of all feces. Many puppies experiment with stool eating but grow out of it.

Poisoning

Poisoning is always a concern with dogs. Signs of poisoning commonly include vomiting, convulsions, staggering, and collapse. If in doubt about whether poison was ingested, call the veterinarian anyway.

If the dog has ingested the poison within the past two hours and is not severely depressed, convulsing, or comatose, you may be advised to induce vomiting (unless the poison was an acid, alkali, petroleum product, solvent, cleaner, or tranquilizer). You can do this by giving hydrogen peroxide (mixed 1:1 with water), salt water, or dry mustard mixed with water.

In other cases, you may be advised to dilute the poison by giving milk, vegetable oil, or egg whites. Activated charcoal can adsorb many toxins. Baking soda or milk of magnesia can be given for ingested acids and vinegar or lemon juice for ingested alkalis.

Ay, Chihuahua!
Poisons

Some all-too-common poisons found in the home and garden and also their effects include the following.

• Ethylene glycol-based antifreeze causes kidney failure. The prognosis is poor once symptoms appear. Veterinary treatment must be obtained within two to four hours of ingestion of even tiny amounts if the dog's life is to be saved.

• Warfarin-based rodent poisons contain anticoagulants that cause uncontrolled internal bleeding. The prognosis ranges from good (if caught soon after ingestion) to poor (if several days have elapsed).

• Cholecalciferol-based rodent poisons deposit calcium into the blood vessels, causing kidney failure and other problems. The prognosis is poor from eating even small amounts.

• Strychnine-based squirrel and bird poisons (usually administered as bird seed with a blue coating of strychnine) can cause seizures, hyperreactivity to noise, and rigid muscles. The prognosis is poor.

• Metaldehyde-based snail and slug poisons cause anxiety, unsteadiness, tremors, coma, and death. The prognosis is fair.

• Arsenic-based insect poisons, weed killers, and wood preservatives cause vomiting, diarrhea, and weakness.
These progress to kidney failure, coma, and death. The prognosis is poor if symptoms have already started.

• Organophosphate-based flea and tick poisons and dewormers, in overdose quantities, can cause vomiting, muscle tremors, pupil constriction, diarrhea, excitability, difficulty breathing, and death. The prognosis varies but can be poor.

• Theobromine (found in chocolate) can cause vomiting, diarrhea, restlessness, fever, seizures, coma, and death. A toxic dose for dogs is 50 mg per pound (per 0.45 kg) of the dog's weight. Dark chocolate contains about 400 mg of theobromine per ounce (per 28.4 g) of chocolate. Therefore, only 0.5 ounces (14.2 g) of dark chocolate could be potentially life threatening to a 4-pound (1.8 kg) dog.

• Lead (found in paint, golf ball coatings, linoleum, and even newsprint) causes abnormal behavior, unsteadiness, seizures, loss of appetite, vomiting, diarrhea, and blindness. The prognosis is usually good.

• Zinc (found in pennies, zinc oxide skin cream, calamine lotion, fertilizers, and shampoos) causes breakdown of red blood cells. Symptoms include decreased appetite, vomiting, diarrhea, depression, pale gums, and brown urine. The prognosis varies.

• Iron-based rose fertilizers can cause kidney and liver failure. A toxic dose is 0.25 teaspoons (1.25 ml) of 5 percent concentration per 5-pound (2.3 kg) dog. The prognosis varies depending upon dosage and treatment delay.

• Onions can cause destruction of red blood cells, especially if large amounts are eaten.

• Many plants are toxic or poisonous. Get to know the ones in your area. Check out *www.aspca.org/pet-care/poison-control/*

• Some other human foods can be toxic; see pages 60–62.

31

rear up and bang his head on the underside of a chair or coffee table, for example.

Your pup naturally explores and part of his exploratory tools are his teeth. Any chewed items left in his wake are your fault, not your pup's—you are the one who should have known better. Harsh corrections are no more effective than a tap on the nose along with a firm *"No"* and removal of the item. If you come across one of your cherished items chewed to bits and feel compelled to lash out, go ahead—hit yourself in the head a few times for slipping up. It may teach you a lesson!

Housebreaking Wees and Woes

Toy dogs have a bad reputation as being among the most difficult of dogs to housebreak. One proposed reason is that their owners tend to give them excessive freedom in the house and that their puddles and piles are so small they are very often deposited unnoticed. Owners may also be hesitant about giving them access to the outdoors, and cold weather makes training them to use the outdoors especially difficult. No reason exists why your Chihuahua (or any toy dog) cannot be housebroken just as readily as any other type of dog, however. You just have to follow some rules, be vigilant, and have realistic expectations.

Your pup will need some time to realize where he should and shouldn't use the bathroom. With some concerted effort, you can speed the process along, but don't expect miracles with puppies. The tales your friends tell you of their wonder pups being housebroken at two months of age are just that—tales. Either that, or you friends are extremely unobservant! Even the best puppies take a lot of time and effort to housebreak. Follow these rules for saving your carpets and creating a housebroken puppy:

Restrict Your Pup's Unsupervised Freedom in the House: All canines have a natural desire to avoid soiling their denning area. The problem is your pup considers only his own bed to be the equivalent of the den, and so he walks a few feet away and eliminates in the middle of your room. By restricting your puppy to an area the size of a wolf's den, such as a crate, when you cannot supervise, you will eliminate this elimination problem. The crate must be small, only large enough to sleep in, for this to work, though. If you provide a crate large enough for your dog to walk away from the end where he sleeps, he can still eliminate outside of his denning area. By placing your little pup into the crate when you can't watch him you will also be ensuring your pup's safety. A tiny Chihuahua baby should never be roaming about unsupervised. Of course, by placing your pup into the crate, you are committing yourself to letting him out regularly. Pups have limited control over their bowels. Unless you let them out when they need to go out, you may force them to eliminate in their own bed. This will not teach them not to wet the bed again. On the contrary, it trains them not to care where they go and not to even try to hold it.

Don't Let Accidents Happen: When puppies have to go, they have to go right now! Puppies have very weak control over their bladder and bowel. If you don't take them to their doggy outhouse often and immediately, they may not be able to avoid soiling. When a pup soils in the house, he labels that area as his bathroom and is likely to go there again. If your pup does have an accident indoors, clean and deodorize the spot thoroughly, and block the pup's access to that area. Learn to predict when your puppy will have to relieve himself:

• Immediately after awakening and soon after heavy drinking or playing, your puppy will urinate.

• Right after eating, or if nervous, your puppy will have to defecate.
• Car rides also tend to elicit defecation—even in the car.
• Circling, whining, sniffing, and generally acting worried usually signal that defecation is imminent.

Know Your Puppy's Limits: Don't expect more from your pup than he is physically able to give. A rule of thumb is that a puppy can, at most, hold his bowels for as many hours as the pup is months old. If the pup is forced to stay confined longer than this limit, you are causing an accident and teaching your pup to go in the wrong place.

Punishment Doesn't Help: Dog owners have been rubbing their dogs' noses in dog mess for years, and it has not been working for years. Dog owners, unfortunately, are slow learners. The dogs trained this way appear to learn just as slowly. Punishing a dog for a mess he made earlier is totally fruitless; it only succeeds in convincing the dog that every once in a while, for no apparent reason, you are apt to go insane and attack. This is a perfect recipe for ruining a trusting relationship. That guilty look you may think your dog is exhibiting is really a look of fear that you have once again lost your mind. Even if you catch your dog in the act, overly enthusiastic correction only teaches the dog not to relieve himself in your presence, even when outside. This doesn't mean you ignore it as your dog ruins your carpet. You can yell *"No! Out!"* and hustle him outside and then reward him for eliminating outside.

Reward Correct Behavior: When the puppy does relieve himself outdoors, heap on the praise and let him know how pleased you are. Adding a food treat really gets the point across. Keep some treats by the door so you are always ready with them.

Go Outside: Most owners think they've done their part by opening the door and pushing the pup outside, but chances are the pup spent his time outside trying to get back inside to his owner. Puppies do not like to be alone. Knowing you are on the other side of the door makes the outdoors unappealing. So you must go outside with the pup every time and be ready to reward him for his good deed.

Indoor Plumbing: Many people have Chihuahuas because they don't have ready access to the outdoors; others find that it's simply convenient to train their dogs to use an indoor potty in addition to going outside. Ranging from simple absorbent pads to self-watering indoor lawns, indoor potties are all the rage for sophisticated Chis.

Paper Training: Newspaper has been the standard indoor system for generations of puppies and even adults. But wet newspaper stinks, falls apart, and tends to stay wet. Dogs can track urine and even newsprint on their wet feet. Other systems really are better.

Litter Boxes: Dogs can be trained to use litter boxes, but you don't want to use cat litter in them. Cat litter is designed to make it easy and enticing for cats to dig—just what you don't want for your dog! It also has a greater tendency to stick to paws and especially to long hair. Finally, dogs are more likely to eat litter, and eating the clumping type of cat litter can be very unhealthy.

Dog litter consists of much larger pellets (about as wide as a pencil and an inch or two in length) made of a mixture of absorbent paper and wood pulp. The pellets allow liquids to drain to the bottom of the pan, and then absorb them from the bottom up, leaving the top layer dry. The litter is placed in a high-sided litter box to accommodate male leg-lifters and dogs that kick after they relieve themselves.

Grid Systems: Grid systems consist of a grating that stands above a paper-lined tray, preventing the dog from stepping in urine or the wet papers just below. The paper is changed as needed.

Disposable Pads: Another solution to keep your dog's feet dry is to increase absorbency with a layer of paper that stays dry. Enter the absorbent pad, based on the same concept as highly absorbent baby diapers. At one time such pads were just considered a replacement for newspaper as a housetraining aid, but as more people found they were handy for everyday use, even with adults, the pads grew in popularity. The best pads have a non-slip waterproof backing, absorbent layers, leak-proof edges, and are scented so that dogs are attracted to them.

Washable Pads: One problem with paper pads is that some dogs, especially puppies, like to turn them into confetti. In addition, because they're disposable, using them exclusively over a period of years can get costly and isn't exactly eco-conscious. Many people look at their expense and opt to just put down a scatter rug for the dog to use. The problem is that dogs then generalize to using all scatter rugs in the house, pretty much defeating the purpose. In addition, scatter rugs can be unwieldy to wash. Other owners just use towels, but towels aren't that absorbent and don't prevent liquids from seeping through to the floor beneath. Besides, who wants to dry off with one after it's been used for that? More savvy owners once bought plastic-lined bed pads made for incontinent people, which trap moisture and don't allow it to seep out. Now, specially made absorbent bed pads are available for dogs. Many breeders of long-coated toy dogs opt to line their kennel run floors with the pads, as they help prevent coat damage that otherwise occurs from urine seeping into the hair.

Sod Systems: Sod systems use either real or artificial grass to provide your dog with a miniature indoor yard. You might think you could hammer together some boards, throw in some dirt, and plant some grass, but after a few weeks, you'd see—or at least smell—the problem with that. In order to thwart odors, you need a waterproof frame (not wood), a way to rinse or drain urine, and an easy means to replace sod periodically. These systems can be kept outside on a balcony or inside (in which case you need to change the grass more often). Otherwise you should replace the grass every couple of months, and in between times spray it twice a week with a urine neutralizer to eliminate odors.

Teaching Your Dog to Use an Indoor Potty: If your dog has never been trained to eliminate outside, training him to use an indoor potty is very simple. You use the same vigilance that you would if you were training him to go outside to relieve himself, except that when he appears ready to go, you hustle him to the indoor area. If the system you're using is pre-scented with odors to attract the dog, he may naturally go there. If the system isn't pre scented, you can capture some urine from your dog and sprinkle it on the area. Dogs tend to relieve themselves where they smell they've gone before.

An indoor pen Is a handy training tool. Place the pen on a tile or nonabsorbent floor, or place a plastic liner, such as an old shower curtain, under it. Put the dog's bed and bowls in one corner, leave a space of a few feet, and cover most of the rest of the floor with your potty system of choice. He won't want to use his bed, so by default he will use the potty. That's why you don't want much bare floor in there, especially at first. If you're using a grid system, take the grid part off at first so he gets used to using the papers beneath. As the dog grows more proficient at hitting the target, you can either expand the pen or, if you're using pads, decrease their area, always keeping them as far away from the bed and bowls as possible. Remember to praise and even give your dog a treat for doing this special "trick."

If your dog is already trained to eliminate outside, you may have to start by bringing in actual sod from his outdoor potty area and placing it on the indoor potty. Place the sod on the indoor system, and gradually decrease the amount of area the sod covers. If you're planning to use artificial grass, and your dog is used to real grass, start with real grass and switch once he's used to going inside.

Despite their convenience, indoor potties are no substitute for taking your dog for a walk. An outdoor excursion is meant as more than an elimination break. It gives your dog exercise, social interaction, mental stimulation, and something to look forward to every day. It does the same for you. But there's no reason you can't have both!

Adult Soiling: No matter how gifted your Chihuahua is, he will probably not be reliably housebroken until 6 to 12 months of age. If an adult continues to eliminate in the house or if a formerly housebroken dog begins to soil, a veterinary examination is warranted. You and your veterinarian will need to consider the following possibilities:

• Older dogs may simply not have the bladder control that they had as youngsters. A doggy door is the best solution.

• Older spayed females may dribble urine, especially when sleeping. Ask your veterinarian about drug therapies.

• Frequent urination of small amounts (especially if the urine is bloody or dark) may indicate an infection of the urinary tract. Such infections must be treated promptly.

• Increased urine production can be a sign of kidney disease or diabetes. Your veterinarian can test for and treat these disorders. Never restrict water from these dogs. A doggy door or litter box is a better way to cope.

• Sometimes a housebroken dog will be forced to soil the house because of a bout of diarrhea and afterward will continue to soil in the same area. If this happens, restrict that area from the dog, deodorize the area with an enzymatic cleaner, and revert to basic housebreaking lessons.

• Male dogs may lift their leg inside of the house as a means of marking it as theirs. Castration will often solve this problem as long as it's performed before the habit has become established. Otherwise, diligent deodorizing and the use of some dog-deterring odorants (available at pet stores) may help.

• Submissive dogs, especially young females, may urinate upon greeting you. Punishment only makes this submissive urination worse. For these dogs, be careful not to bend over or otherwise dominate them. Keep greetings calm. Submissive urination is usually outgrown as the dog gains more confidence.

• Some dogs defecate or urinate due to the stress of separation anxiety. You must treat the anxiety to cure the symptom. Dogs that mess their crate when left in it are usually suffering from separation anxiety or anxiety about being closed in a crate. Other telltale signs of anxiety-produced elimination are drooling, scratching, and escape-oriented behavior. You need to treat separation anxiety and start crate training over, placing the dog into it for a short period of time and gradually working up to longer times. Dogs that suffer from crate claustrophobia but not separation anxiety do better if left loose in a dog-proofed room or yard.

Home Destruction

How much damage can a little Chihuahua do? Ask the owner of a Chihuahua with separation anxiety. One of the joys of living with a Chihuahua is the hero's welcome you can expect whenever you return home. One of the aggravations can be the state of your home upon your return. Some Chihuahuas have spent the time you were away practicing their redecorating skills. To a dog, redecorating and destroying are synonymous. Sometimes they destroy because of boredom; other times they destroy because they love you.

Unruly Behavior: Before discussing how your dog destroying your home is a token of his love for you, look at the times when this behavior is not. Puppies are natural demolition dogs. They vandalize for the sheer ecstasy that only a search-and-destroy mission can provide.

Most Chihuahua owners appreciate the entertainment that their little dogs, even at their wildest, provide. Despite their popular image as lap dogs, Chihuahuas are energetic, inquisitive dogs. Their bodies may be small, but they still need exercise— and their brains need even more stimulation. The best cure for an overactive Chihuahua is lots of mental and physical exercise. This means a short walk, small adventure, challenging obedience lesson, or fun game at least once a day and more often for younger or more active dogs. A dog agility course is a great mind and body exerciser. A variety of toys, given only when the dog is to be left alone, can also help fend off destruction of your valuables.

Anxious Behavior: When calm adults destroy your home, they may be upset at being left alone. They are not destroying out of spite, as is too often assumed, but out of anxiety. Being left alone is an extremely stressful situation for these highly social animals. They react by becoming agitated and trying to escape from confinement. Perhaps they reason that if they can just get out of the house, they will be reunited with their people. The telltale sign of dogs suffering from this separation anxiety is that most of their destructive behavior is focused around doors and windows. Punishing these dogs is ineffective because it actually increases the anxiety level of the dogs, since they both come to look forward to and dread the owner's return.

Keeping the dog confined in a crate may save your home but seldom

deals with the problem. Some dogs become so anxious at being placed into the crate that they need to undergo behavior modification every bit as much as dogs that are allowed the run of the house. Such dogs often urinate or defecate in their crate, rip up bedding, dig and bite at the crate door, bark, pant, shake, and drool. The same is true of locking them in the bathroom. Many dogs are upset by close confinement and do better if they are kept in a room with baby gates or in an exercise pen.

Separation anxiety should be treated like any other fear—by working slowly and preventing the dog from becoming upset. This is done by leaving the dog alone for very short periods of time and gradually working to longer periods, taking care never to allow the dog to become anxious during any session. When you must leave your dog for long periods during the conditioning program, leave him in a different part of the house than the one in which the conditioning sessions take place. This way you won't undo all of your work if the dog becomes over-stressed by your long absence.

When you return home, no matter how horrified or relieved you are at the condition of the house, greet your dog calmly. Then have him perform a simple trick or obedience exercise so that you have an excuse to praise him. In severe cases, your veterinarian can prescribe antianxiety medications to help your pet deal with being left alone. These medications are most useful when combined with the gradual desensitization techniques outlined previously. A lot of patience and often a whole lot of self-control are needed, but it's not fair to you or your dog to let this situation continue. It will only get worse.

Barking: Some Chihuahuas bark more than others. Most owners appreciate the dog that barks when somebody comes to the door; few appreciate one that barks at his own shadow. If your dog will not stop barking when you tell him to, distract him with a loud noise of your own. Begin to anticipate when your dog will start barking, distract him, and reward him for quiet behavior. You will actually create a better watchdog by discouraging your dog from barking at nonthreatening objects and encouraging him to bark at suspicious people. Allow your Chihuahua to bark momentarily at strangers. Then call your dog to you and praise him for quiet behavior, distracting him with an obedience exercise if need be.

Isolated dogs will often bark through frustration or as a means of getting attention and alleviating loneliness. Even if the attention gained includes punishment, they continue to bark in order to obtain the temporary presence of the owner. The fault is not theirs; they should never have been banned to solitary confinement in the first place.

The simplest solution is to move the dog's quarters to a less-isolated location. If barking occurs when you put your dog to bed, move his bed

into your bedroom or condition your dog by rewarding him for successively longer periods of quiet behavior. The distraction of a special chew toy, given only at bedtime, may help alleviate barking. Remember, a sleeping dog cannot bark, so exercise can be a big help by tiring your Chihuahua.

The Sociable Chihuahua

Even if you live by yourself, your Chihuahua needs to be ready to meet new people, dogs, and other animals. At the same time, you need to be aware of any special dangers they might pose to your dog.

Chihuahuas and Children: Many children are drawn to Chihuahuas because Chihuahuas are irresistibly cute. Carrying a little Chihuahua around, playing games such as tag, fetch, and maybe even dress up are fun. Children can get carried away, however. Sometimes they do not realize that only one mistake can permanently injure or even kill a tiny Chihuahua. Any child who interacts with any dog, but especially a Chihuahua, needs to be thoroughly schooled in dog safety and responsibility. Children must be taught that Chihuahuas cannot be dropped, hit in the head, encouraged to jump off furniture, stepped on, fallen upon, or yanked off the ground in a overly vigorous game of tug-of-war. This requires some restraint and forethought on the part of the child, and many young children are not capable of that. Children and Chihuahuas should always be supervised when together. They can eventually become the very best of buddies—but you need to guide them so they can both grow up healthy and safe together.

Some Chihuahuas are afraid of children either because they don't understand what children are or because they have had bad experiences with children. Introduce dogs and children carefully, encouraging each child to be gentle and to offer the dog a treat. Do not allow young children to run around and possibly fall onto the dog or to pull his hair, ears, or tail. Allowing children to abuse a Chihuahua is not fair to even the most saintly of dogs.

Chihuahuas and Babies: Many devoted dog owners have been known to get rid of their dogs when a new baby comes home often because of the stories they've heard about what dogs can do to babies. No reason exists why your Chihuahua and baby cannot grow up respecting and loving each other.

When bringing the baby home from the hospital, first let the dog get used to the sound and odor of the new family member. Have the dog sit and stay, bring the baby into the room, and reward the dog for staying. Gradually move the baby closer, all the while rewarding the dog for his good behavior. Always praise and pet the dog when the baby is present. Never shuttle the dog out of the room because the baby is coming in. You want the dog to associate the baby with good things coming, not be jealous or resentful. Remember, your Chihuahua probably used to be the baby of the family.

Chihuahuas and Other Pets: Your Chihuahua may be small, but in his heart he is a wolf. He will love chasing cats and small animals. The problem is, they may end up chasing him! A cat scratch can do considerable damage to vulnerable Chihuahua eyes, so you must introduce your dogs and cats carefully. Feed them together, and don't allow either one to run after or from the other. Make sure other, more entertaining things are available to distract your Chihuahua. Once they get used to one another, Chihuahuas and cats can become close friends.

Chihuahuas and Wildlife: In some parts of the country, small dogs and cats have been caught and eaten by wildlife. Be familiar with the wildlife in your area, and take precautions to make sure either that they cannot get into your yard or that you are always outside when your Chihuahua is. A Chihuahua puppy is not too large for a bird of prey to swoop down and fly away with him. In fact, even adult Chihuahuas may fall victim to large birds. A screened porch is a good safety precaution in some parts of

the country. Coyotes have also been known to attack small dogs. Once again, a Chihuahua owner must be extra vigilant.

Chihuahuas and Other Dogs: Many Chihuahuas don't seem to know they are small, at least when it comes to their interactions with other dogs. They run up to any dog they see and challenge him with all the cockiness they can muster. Sometimes this tough front is enough to scare away big dogs (which may have been the Chihuahua's plan in the first place—the best defense is a strong offense). However, sometimes the other dog meets the challenge. No matter how tough your Chihuahua is, he's not going to win in a real fight against a big dog.

Not all big dogs need to be provoked, however. Wherever you take your Chihuahua, you must be on the lookout for dogs that could view your Chihuahua as a prey animal. Many breeds of dogs were bred to run down and catch or kill any small, fast-moving mammal. By the time they realize they've caught another dog, it could be too late. Never let your Chihuahua off lead where big dogs are running loose.

Aggression toward strange dogs is a biologically normal trait of canines but one that is not suitable for dogs in today's world. A dog naturally defends his home territory against strange dogs. Many dogs believe their home territory extends into the street in front of their home, which can spell danger if you are walking your Chihuahua down the street. If you walk your dog in a neighborhood with dogs that run loose, you must

take steps to ensure your dog's safety from attacking dogs. This may include carrying a little protective dog carrier, a big stick, or pepper spray. One reason using a harness is a good idea when walking your Chihuahua is that pulling your dog away from danger and even into your arms is a lot easier by his chest rather than neck.

Your own Chihuahua can be the dog that runs into the street defending his home turf. This is why no Chihuahua should be allowed to wander around in the front yard. He could be struck by a car, or the dog he's barking at could just bite back.

When introducing new dogs, the dogs should meet on neutral territory and have a mutual distraction. Going for a long walk together in a new area, with each dog held on leash, is an ideal way for dogs to get used to one another and associate the other with a pleasurable event. Try to prevent a dog that tends to be aggressive from marking with urine during the walk. Because male dogs mark their territory by urinating on various posts, the more you allow a dog to mark, the more likely that dog will behave aggressively toward other dogs in that area.

Most Chihuahua housemates get along together very well. Problems between housemates are more likely to occur between dogs of the same sex and same age. Seniority counts for a lot in the dog world, and a young pup will usually grow up respecting his elders. Sometimes, a youngster gets aspirations to be top dog, however, or two dogs of about the same age never quite decide which one is leadership material. Then the trouble starts. Remember to decide first if this is natural rough play behavior between the two. An occasional disagreement, too, is normal. A disagreement that draws blood, leaves one dog screaming, or in which the two dogs cannot be separated is a potential problem. Repeated disagreements spell trouble. Neutering one or both males in a two-male dominance battle can sometimes help, but spaying females seldom helps.

Human nature says to soothe the underdog and punish the bully. However, that would be doing the underdog the worst favor you could. If your dogs are fighting for dominance, they are doing so in part because in the dog world, the dominant dog gets the lion's share of the most precious resources. You and your attention are the very most precious resources your dog can have. If you now give your attention to the loser, the winner will try only harder to beat the daylights out of the loser so your attention will go where it should go—to the winner. You will do your losing dog the best favor if you treat the winning dog like a king and the losing dog like a prince. This means you always greet, pet, and feed the top dog first. Doing so goes against human nature, but it goes with dog nature.

When Chihuahuas Bite: Although imagining packs of vicious Chihuahuas marauding the countryside is hard, some Chihuahuas do actually bite. In fact, Chihuahuas have a reputation as nippers among some groups of people. Even though they aren't exactly man killers, they can certainly be frightening and they can break the skin. Why would this be so?

First of all, most Chihuahuas do not bite. Those that do bite usually do so for a couple of reasons. One reason is that they tend to be sheltered by their owners and aren't properly socialized when young. Chihuahuas are not social butterflies. Most of them prefer the company of their special person or family and aren't thrilled about getting touched by a stranger. Others are uneasy around strangers. And many Chihuahuas are protective of their special person. They consider their person's lap their private territory. Very often

their owner is holding them when they meet strange people. The stranger then reaches to pet the dog, and the dog nips either in fear and self-defense or in defense of his owner and territory. From the dog's point of view, a giant is invading his personal space and threatening his—or his owner's—well-being. Compound this with the fact that many irresponsible or unknowledgeable breeders excuse or ignore this behavior, and so fail to select for nonbiting temperaments, and you can have a problem.

The best solution is prevention. One means is to make sure the parents of your prospective dog are not inclined to bite. Most dogs from show and obedience lines are selected from generations of amiable Chihuahuas because these dogs must

constantly interact with strangers when competing. Those that bite are disqualified. The second means of prevention is early socialization, exposing your Chihuahua pup to kind strangers. The third means of prevention is trying to see things from your Chihuahua's perspective. Do not allow strangers to bear down on him, reach for him, or try to pick him up. Strangers really don't need to pet your dog unless he wants to be petted. If

you need to hand your dog to someone, such as a veterinarian, hand the dog rear first so that he is reassured by looking toward you. Don't excuse biting behavior, but don't place your dog into a situation where biting seems like the best alternative.

Recognizing Aggression: Many types of aggression can occur in dogs, and the treatment for them can be very different. Puppies and dogs play by growling and biting. Usually they play with their littermates this way. However, if yours is an only puppy, you will just have to do. So many people have heard horror stories about dogs that when their pup growls and bites, they immediately label him as a problem biter. You need to know the difference between true aggression and playful aggression. Look for these clues that tell you it's all in good fun:
• Wagging tail
• Down on elbows in front, with the rump in the air (the play-bow position)
• Barks intermingled with growls
• Lying down or rolling over
• Bounding leaps or running in circles
• Mouthing or chewing on you or other objects

On the other hand, look for these clues to know that you better watch out:
• Low growl combined with a direct stare
• Tail held stiffly
• Sudden, unpredictable bites
• Growling or biting in defense of food, toys, or bed
• Growling or biting in response to punishment

Chances are your Chihuahua is simply playing. Still, this doesn't mean you should let him use you as a pin cushion. Those little puppy teeth are sharp! When your pup bites you, simply say *"Ouch! No!"* and remove your hand from his mouth. Replace your hand with a toy. If he doesn't get the message, just walk away and ignore him. Slapping your dog is uncalled for—he was just trying to play and meant no harm. Slapping is also a form of aggression that could give your dog the idea that he had better try (bite) harder next time because you're playing the game a lot rougher. You don't want to encourage playful aggression, but you don't want to punish it. You want to redirect it.

Aggression Toward Humans: Treatment of aggression starts with deciding what kind of aggression it is. Dominance aggression is far more rare than most people believe. More common are resource-guarding aggression, territorial aggression, and fear aggression. Treating for the wrong type of aggression may simply make matters worse. Regardless of the type of aggression, something that is always counterproductive is the alpha roll, in which you roll the dog over on his back and hold him there. It was based on a faulty interpretation of wolf behavior and is likely to make a fearful dog worse, and also to get you bitten! For cases of aggression, your best course of action is to consult a veterinary behaviorist.

Shyness: If the dog is afraid of people, do not let people push themselves onto him. Doing so frightens the dog, sometimes to the extent that the person could be bitten. Shy dogs are like shy people in some ways. They are not so much afraid of people as they are afraid of being the center of people's attention. Strangers should be asked to ignore shy dogs, even when approached by the dog. When the dog gets braver, have the stranger offer him a tidbit, at first while not even looking at the dog. Your dog does not need to love strangers. However, he should be comfortable enough with them so that he can be treated by a veterinarian, boarded, or caught if lost without being emotionally traumatized.

When Chihuahuas Get Scared

Even the bravest of Chihuahuas can sometimes develop illogical fears, or phobias. The most common are fears of strange people or dogs and of gunshots or thunder. Every once in a while, a particularly imaginative

Small Talk
Chihuahua Talk

Despite being dubbed man's best friend, the relationship between human and dog is one-sided. People expect their dogs to understand them, seldom bothering to try to learn the dog's language. With very little effort, you can meet your Chihuahua halfway and learn to speak Chihuahuaese.

Living with a Chihuahua is like having a wolf in the house—sort of. As much as they have shaken off their wild vestiges, Chihuahuas still speak the ancestral language of wolves.

• A wagging tail and lowered head upon greeting is a sign of submission.

• A lowered body, tucked rear, urination, and perhaps even rolling over is a sign of extreme submission.

• A yawn is often a sign of nervousness. Drooling and panting can indicate extreme nervousness (as well as car sickness).

• Exposed teeth, raised hackles, very upright posture, stiff-legged gait, and direct stare indicate very dominant behavior.

• Elbows on the ground and rear in the air is the classic play-bow position and is an invitation for a game.

Chihuahua will come up with a bizarre fear all his own, but this can usually be treated using the same general concepts that will be described.

The cardinal rule of working with a fearful dog is never to push him into situations that might overwhelm him. Some people erroneously think the best way to deal with a scared dog is to inundate him with the very thing he's afraid of until he gets used to that object, sound, or person. This concept (called *flooding*) does not work because the dog is usually so terrified, he never gets over the fear enough to realize the situation is safe.

Other owners tend to try to reassure their Chihuahua by petting or holding him when scared. This only reinforces the behavior and often also convinces the dog that the owner is frightened as well. You want to maintain a jolly attitude and make your dog work for praise. The first step is to teach your dog a few simple commands. Performing these exercises correctly gives you a reason to praise your Chihuahua and also increases his sense of security because he knows what is expected of him.

In some cases, the dog is petrified at even the lowest level of exposure to whatever he is scared of. You may have to use antianxiety drugs in conjunction with training to calm your dog enough to make progress. This is when you need the advice of a behaviorist.

Noise Phobias: Fear of thunder or gunshots are common problems in older dogs. To see a normally confident Chihuahua quivering and panting in the closet at the slight rumblings of a distant thunderstorm is a sad sight that only worsens with time. The time to do something about this phobia is at the first sign of trouble. Try to avoid fostering these fears. Act cheerful when a thunderstorm strikes. Play with your dog, or give him a tidbit. Once a dog develops a noise phobia, try to find a recording of that noise. Play it at a very low level, and reward your dog for calm behavior. Gradually increase the intensity and duration of the recording. A program of gradual desensitization, with the dog exposed to the frightening person or thing and then rewarded for calm behavior, is time consuming but the best way to alleviate any fear. Again, calming drugs may be helpful during training but should not become a crutch.

Small Indiscretions

As with people, even Chihuahuas can develop an astounding array of behavioral problems. They may look like angels, and they may even act like angels most of the time, but even the best Chihuahuas sometimes do the worst things. Sometimes they don't know better, and sometimes they can't help themselves. These dogs need you to teach them better, and they need you to help them help themselves. Until recently, even the best owners had little choice of where to turn for advice for dog behavioral problems. Well-meaning but misguided training advice from friends, breeders, or even veterinarians or dog trainers without a

scientific background in dog behavior too often only made things worse. Too many Chihuahuas have been relinquished because their owners simply never were given the proper advice to deal with their dogs' behavioral problems. Great strides have been made in recent years in canine behavioral therapy. Qualified behaviorists will consider both behavioral and medical therapies. As a first step in any serious behavioral problem, a thorough veterinary exam should be performed.

No dog, and no owner, is perfect. Our dogs seldom act and do exactly as we would wish them to; we probably let them down even more. We try to change what we can, gripe about the rest, and love them regardless because the good more than makes up for the bad.

Chapter Four

A Good Mind to Do Something

Even Chihuahuas need to be trained. A well-trained dog is a safer and happier dog. Around the house you may need your dog to stay while you leave the door open for a moment, to sit out of the way while you prepare his dinner, to lie down while you groom him, or to come when you call. Dog training is not a matter of making a servant out of your dog—after all, no self-respecting Chihuahua would stand for that. Instead, training should be a way of strengthening the bond between you and your dog by helping your dog understand what you are trying to tell him. When you train your dog the right way, both of you will look forward to spending a special time of learning together. Your job is to make training exciting and rewarding, incorporating play and using lots of toys and treats for rewards.

The Training Game

Chihuahuas learn best both when they are thinking and when they are having fun. That's why the old-fashioned methods using force training make for slow progress—or none at all. The best Chihuahua trainers know how to make training into a challenging, but always winnable, game.

Despite their size, Chihuahuas can be tough. They don't like being pushed around, and they are apt to respond to such insulting methods with defiance. In the old days when force-training methods were the accepted way, such dogs were labeled as stubborn and stupid. Professional trainers knew better. They could train such dogs to do just about anything because they didn't use force-training methods. They knew that to get a thinking dog to do what you wanted, it also had to be what the dog wanted. One way to do that is with the use of food and play as rewards.

Food as Reward: Professional animal trainers and animal-learning scientists have shown that food training is highly effective. Food is used initially to guide the dog and later as a reward. The dog is then gradually weaned from getting a food reward for each correct response but, instead, is rewarded only at random correct responses. This random pay-off is the same psychology very effectively used to induce people to put money (the correct response) into slot machines.

Timing: Great dog trainers have great timing. The crux of training is anticipation. A dog comes to anticipate that after hearing a command, he will be rewarded if he performs some action, and he will eventually perform this action without further assistance from you. Your timing is everything. Remember the following sequence:

1. Name: Alert your dog that your next words are directed toward him by preceding commands with his name.

2. Command: Always use the same word in the same tone.

3. Action: Don't simultaneously place the dog into position as you say the command, which negates the predictive value of the command. Instead, give the dog time to assimilate your command, then get him to perform the desired action.

4. Reward: As soon as possible after the dog has performed correctly should come a signal *("Good!")* followed by a reward.

The sooner a reward follows an action, the better the association. Rewarding a dog instantly is often difficult. You can do the next best thing by immediately signaling the dog a reward is coming. The best way to do this is with a noticeable

sound the dog does not otherwise hear in everyday life, such as a special word or sound. This special signal is given immediately after the correct action and just before the reward.

In summary, the proper timing sequence would be *"Dinky"* — pause — *"Sit"* — pause — (get him to sit) — special signal — (give him the treat).

Basic Training

Educating your Chihuahua can never begin too early or too late. With a very young pup, train for even shorter time periods than you would an adult. The exercises every Chi-

Small Talk
Tools of the Trade

The secret of training is not in the tools; it's in the trainer. Still, having the right tools can make things go a bit easier. Basic training equipment usually includes both short (6-foot or 1.8 m) and long (about 20-foot or 6.1 m) lightweight leads and a collar. Traditionally, a choke collar has been used. However, many trainers prefer a buckle collar for training Chihuahuas.

A special Chihuahua-training tool that some people find handy is a solid leash. This is a hollow, lightweight tube the leash can be strung through. This is handy for teaching heeling so that you can guide your dog better. Otherwise, when you pull on the leash it just pulls upward. With the solid leash, you can direct the pull in one direction or another. Getting this to work properly does take some practice, however. In addition, many dogs are skittish about a stick that seems to hover over their head. Thus, the solid lead does not work for all trainers or dogs.

Another Chihuahua tool is a lightweight stick you can use to point to where you want your Chihuahua to face. You do this by giving your dog a bit of food when he touches the end of the stick with his nose. Then, once he has the hang of that, you can guide his nose (along with the rest of his body, which must follow) by moving the stick. Other trainers prefer to use the stick as an extension for their own hands so they can gently tap (not hit!) or guide the dogs into position without bending over every time.

huahua should eventually know are *sit, down, stay, come,* and *heel.* These exercises will be demonstrated with the help of a budding Chihuahua genius named Dinky.

First, you have to get Dinky's attention. Say *"Dinky, watch me."* When he looks in your direction, say *"Good!"* and give him a treat or other reward. Gradually require Dinky to look at you for longer and longer periods before rewarding him.

Come: If Dinky learns only one command, that command should be to come when called. Obeying could save his life. He probably already knows how to come. After all, he comes when called for dinner. You want him to respond to *"Dinky, come"* with that same enthusiasm. In other words, *come* should always be associated with good things.

Have a helper gently restrain Dinky while you back away and entice him until he is struggling to get to you. Then excitedly call *"Dinky, come!"* and turn and run away. Your helper should immediately release him. When Dinky catches you, give him a special reward. Always keep up a jolly attitude and make him feel lucky to be part of such a wonderful game.

Next let Dinky meander around. In the midst of his investigations, call, run backward, and reward him when he runs to you. If Dinky ignores you, attach a light line to him and give him a very gentle tug to guide him to you immediately after you call. After a few repetitions, drop the long line, let him mosey around a bit, then call. If he begins to come, run away and let him chase you as part of the game. If he does not come, pick up the line and give a tug, then run away as usual.

As Dinky becomes more reliable, you should begin to practice (still on the long line) in the presence of distractions. Hold onto his leash just in case the distractions prove too enticing.

Some dogs develop a habit of dancing around just out of your reach, considering your futile grabs to be another part of this wonderful game. You can prevent this by requiring Dinky to allow you to hold him by the collar before you reward him. Eventually, you may add sitting in front of you as part of the game. In an obedience trial, a dog must sit in front of you within touching distance in order to pass the recall exercise. Points are deducted for not sitting directly in front of you. In real life, however, you just want him to come!

Sit: *Sit* is the prototypical dog command and with good reason. It's a simple way to control your dog, and it's easy. The simplest way to teach the *sit* is to hold a tidbit just above Dinky's eye level while he is standing. Say *"Dinky, sit,"* and then move the tidbit toward him until it is slightly behind and above his eyes. You may have to keep a hand on his rump to prevent him from jumping up. When he begins to look up and bend his hind legs, say *"Good!"* then offer the tidbit. Repeat this, requiring him to bend his legs more and more until he must be sitting before receiving the *"Good!"* and the reward. If Dinky backs up instead of sits down,

place his rear against a wall while training.

Stay: Many dogs have the dangerous habit of bolting through open doors. This can be especially dangerous for a little dog, which could be caught in a slamming door or encounter outdoor dangers once through the door. Teach your dog to sit and stay until given the release signal before walking through any door.

Have Dinky sit, then say *"Stay"* in a soothing voice. You can omit the dog's name here because many dogs jump up in anticipation when they hear their name—the opposite of the goal of the *stay*. If he tries to get up or lie down, gently but instantly place him back into position. Work up to a few seconds, give a release word (*"OK!"*), praise, and reward. Next, step out (starting with your right foot), and turn to stand directly in front of Dinky while he stays. Staring into your dog's eyes as if hypnotizing

him to stay is tempting, but this really will have the opposite effect! Staring is perceived by the dog as a threat. It can be intimidating, causing the dog to squirm out of position and come to you, his leader! Work up to longer times, but do not ask a young puppy to stay longer than 30 seconds. The object is not to push your dog to the limit but to let him succeed. Finally, practice with the dog on lead by the front door or in the car. For a reward, take Dinky for a walk.

Down: When you need Dinky to stay in one place for a long time, you can't expect him to sit or stand. This is when the *down* command really comes in handy.

Begin teaching the *down* command with the dog in the sitting position. Say *"Dinky, down."* Then show him a tidbit, and move it below his nose toward the ground. If he reaches down to get it, give it to him. Repeat, requiring Dinky to reach farther down (without lifting his rear from the ground) until he has to lower his elbows to the ground. This is easier if he is on a raised surface and

Small Talk
Training on High

Teach stationary exercises, like *sit, down,* and *stay* on a raised surface. This allows you to have eye contact with your dog and gives you a better vantage from which to help your dog learn. It also helps keep your little one from being distracted and taking off to play. Of course, make sure your dog cannot jump off and hurt himself!

you lower the tidbit below the level of that surface, so he is peering over the edge. Never try to cram him into the *down* position, which can scare a submissive dog and cause a dominant dog to resist. Practice the *down/ stay* just as you did the *sit/stay.*

Heel: A pup's first experience walking on leash should be positive. Use a very lightweight lead; a show lead is ideal. Never drag a reluctant pup or let him hit the end of the lead. Start by coaxing him a few steps at a time with food. When he follows you, praise and reward. In this way, he begins to realize that following you while walking on lead brings rewards.

Once your pup is prancing alongside, ask a little more of him. Even if you have no intention of teaching a perfect competition *heel,* Dinky should know how to walk politely at your side.

Have Dinky sit in *heel* position; that is, on your left side with his neck next to and parallel with your leg. If you line up your feet and your dog's front feet, that's close enough. Say *"Dinky, heel,"* and step off with your left foot first. During your first few practice sessions, keep him on a short lead, holding him in *heel* position, and of course praising him. The traditional method of letting him lunge to the end of the lead and then snapping him back is unfair to any dog if you have not first shown him what you expect. This is dangerous for a Chihuahua in any event. Instead, after a few sessions of showing him *heel* position, give him a

Small Talk
Recall Rule

Never have your Chihuahua come to you and then scold him for something he's done. In your dog's mind you are scolding him for coming, not for any earlier misdeed.

little more loose lead and use a tidbit or your long aiming stick to guide Dinky into the correct position.

If Dinky still forges ahead after you have shown him what is expected, stop dead in your tracks. Don't pull back; just stand there. Only when he lets the leash go slack do you say *"Good!"* and reward or move forward. Practice this until he stops pulling as soon as you stop. Next walk toward something he wants to reach. If he pulls, stop or even back up. The point is not to jerk your dog back, but to show him that pulling gets him there more slowly. When he stops pulling, go toward the goal again. The goal is his reward, but the only way he can reach it is to stop pulling! Never jerk your dog or let him hit the end of the leash or do anything that could possibly hurt his

Small Talk
Starting Off on the
Right Foot (or Left)

By stepping off with your right foot when you want your dog to stay and your left foot when you want your dog to heel, you will give your little dog an eye-level cue about what you are saying.

neck. Some Chihuahuas are predisposed to tracheal collapse, and such rough techniques could precipitate problems.

Keep up a normal pace that requires your dog to walk fairly briskly. Too slow a pace gives him time to sniff and sightsee. A brisk pace will focus his attention upon you. Add some about-faces, right and left turns, and walking at different speeds. Teach Dinky to sit every time you stop. Vary your routine to combat boredom. Be sure to give the *"OK"* command before allowing Dinky to sniff, forge, and meander on lead.

Higher Education

If you think obedience titles may be in your future, you might as well think big. Advanced obedience titles are well within the reach of Chihuahuas, who often relish the chance to do more active exercises than those involved in basic obedience. Many trainers find the best time to teach the advanced exercises is in the beginning. So rather than wait until your dog has earned the Novice degree, you may wish to introduce retrieving and jumping now.

Several advanced exercises require high and broad jumping. Use only extremely low jumps when working with a puppy. These exercises also require retrieving special obedience dumbbells and gloves. So get these items now while your Chihuahua is more likely to want to carry things in his mouth. Even more advanced exercises will involve hand signals and scent discrimination. Again, don't postpone introducing these concepts to your dog. Teach hand signals just as you would voice signals. If your dog already knows voice signals, immediately precede your standard voice command with a hand signal.

For scent discrimination, get your dog used to using his nose to find hidden objects with your scent on them. Throw a scented object in the midst of several unscented objects that are tied down. Your dog will learn that he cannot pick up the articles without your scent. Be careful you do not contaminate the other objects with your scent by touching them.

Many Chihuahuas find the basic obedience exercises boring, so teaching advanced exercises along with basic ones can help keep your dog's enthusiasm high. Another way to keep up enthusiasm is with fun dog tricks. Tricks are easy to teach with the help of the same obedience concepts outlined in the training section. Try these standards:

• Teach *roll over* by telling your dog to lie down. First say *"Roll over,"* and then lure him over onto his side with a treat. Once the dog reliably rolls onto his side, use the treat to guide him onto his back. Then guide him the rest of the way, eventually giving the treat only when he has rolled all the way over.

• Teach *catch* by tossing a tidbit or a ball into a high arc over your dog's face. If he misses, snatch the tidbit off the ground before the dog can reach it. Eventually, he'll realize that to beat you to the bounty, he'll have to grab it before it reaches the ground.

• Teach *shake hands* by having your dog sit. Say *"Shake,"* and hold a treat in your closed hand in front of your dog. Many dogs will pick up a foot to paw at your hand. These are the naturals! You have to give others a little nudge on the leg or lure their heads far to one side so they have to lift the leg up on the opposite side. As soon as the paw leaves the ground, reward! Then require your dog to lift it higher and longer.

• Teach *speak* by saying *"Speak"* when it appears your Chihuahua is about to bark. Then reward. Do not reward barking unless you have first said *"Speak."*

Of course, the best tricks are the ones unique to your dog. If your Chihuahua has an endearing behavior, make up a cute command word or phrase. Slip it in when your dog looks like he's going to be doing his trick and give your dog a good reward when he does the trick. It may be the first step to fame!

Small Talk
The Rules

• Guide, do not force. Forcing Chihuahuas can cause them to resist, actually slowing down learning.
• Once is enough. Repeating a command over and over or shouting it louder and louder never helped any dog understand what was expected.
• Give your dog a hunger for learning. Your Chihuahua will work better if his stomach is not full and will be more responsive to food rewards. Never try to train a sleepy, tired, or hot dog.
• Be a quitter. You, and your dog, have good days and bad days. On bad days, quit. Never train your dog when you are irritable or impatient. Even on good days, don't push. After about 15 minutes, your dog's performance will begin to suffer unless a lot of play is involved. Keep your Chihuahua wanting more.
• The best laid plans don't include dogs. Nothing ever goes as perfectly as it does in training instructions. Although setbacks may occur, you can train your Chihuahua as long as you remember to be consistent, firm, gentle, realistic, and patient.

The Good Chihuahua Citizen

Part of the fun of owning a Chihuahua is showing him off in public. These little dogs attract attention wherever you go, and people have a hard time not stopping to pet or ask about your dog. While this can be a great deal of fun and a wonderful way to meet people, it won't be much fun if your dog barks or snarls at everyone he meets. Such behavior will reflect badly on the Chihuahua breed.

Unfortunately, many dogs of all breeds behave poorly in public. Your dog does not have to be an obedience whiz to act civilized, but some rudimentary manners are required. In fact, the most magnificent champion in the show or obedience ring is no credit to his breed if he is not a good public citizen in the real world. In order to encourage and formally recognize dogs that behave in public, the AKC offers the Canine Good Citizen (CGC) certificate. This requires your Chihuahua to:
• Accept a friendly stranger who greets you.
• Sit politely for petting by a stranger.
• Allow a stranger to pet and groom him.
• Walk politely on a loose lead.
• Walk through a crowd on a lead.
• Sit and lie down on command and stay in place while on a 20-foot (6 m) line.
• Come when called.
• React politely to another dog.
• React calmly to distractions.

• Remain in place calmly when held by a stranger for three minutes in the owner's absence.

Class Acts

Good obedience classes are great aids for training your dog to behave properly at home, in public, and in competition. To find a good class, get referrals from other small-dog trainers, and sit in on the class. If the class uses outdated yank-and-jerk methods, look elsewhere. Your friend's well-being is worth too much.

If you think you would like to enter obedience trials (see page 148), a class is a necessity. Obedience trials are held amid great distractions. It would be nearly impossible for your dog to pass without having some experience working around other dogs. Obedience classes are filled with people who share many of your interests. If you take the plunge into competition, class is a place to celebrate wins and laugh about failures.

Sometimes your Chihuahua will be the star pupil. Sometimes he will be the class dunce. Each dog will progress at his own pace. Every dog will improve, and many dogs will profit from repeating the same class after using the first time through as a warm-up. Some dogs are too excited, or too nervous, the first time through to concentrate properly on their lesson.

Your Chihuahua is smart. After all, Chihuahuas have the largest brain compared to body size of any breed. Exercise your Chihuahua's brain power; you may be in for a surprise!

Chapter Five
Chihuahua Chow Time

Every day you place a bowl down in front of your dog filled with food that influences his performance, health, and longevity, as well as dining pleasure. While the same can be said of humans' meals, dog diets differ from human diets in that most dogs are usually fed only a single type of food day in and day out. This makes choosing the best diet even more important, intimidating, and controversial.

Chihuahua owners have even less room to experiment with their dogs. A small snack that would be inconsequential to a large dog could make up a significant portion of a tiny dog's diet. This means you have to be especially vigilant about what you feed your Chihuahua. Fortunately, because Chihuahua portions are small, you can afford to splurge on the very best-quality foods on the market or even make your own.

The Natural Versus Processed Food Controversy

For thousands of years, wild canids ate a diet consisting largely of raw meat as well as whatever vegetables were contained in their prey's stomach contents. Early domesticated dogs subsisted largely on human garbage as well as on whatever they could catch or forage themselves. For many centuries, domestic dogs ate mostly leftovers, scraps, and bread products. Only in recent decades have commercial foods been available, complete with testing of their nutritional value. Proponents of commercial foods point out that these diets have been constantly adjusted and tested on generations of dogs to provide optimal nutrition and that premium-grade foods contain quality ingredients acceptable for human consumption. Critics of commercial foods point out that these foods are highly processed, do not resemble a dog's natural diet, are not fresh, and may use ingredients unfit for human consumption.

Raw-Food Diets: A recently popularized alternative to commercial diets is the family of raw food diets. These diets advocate more natural feeding by giving dogs whole raw animal carcasses, particularly chicken, which the dogs eat, bones and all. Proponents point out that such diets are more like the natural diet of ancestral dogs and claim good health, clean teeth, and economical food bills. Controlled studies concerning the safety and efficacy of such diets have yet to be published.

Detractors point out that, while the raw diet may be closer to what wolves eat, dogs are no longer wolves and have not lived off the land for thousands of generations. In addition, many people have oversimplified these diets and commonly feed a diet of chicken wings exclusively, which is neither natural nor balanced. Critics also worry that raw foods from processing plants may contain the bacteria salmonella and Escherichia coli, although dogs are more resistant to illness from them compared with people. If raw food is fed, it should be only fresh and locally processed. Chihuahuas seem especially poor candidates for these diets. They certainly can no longer claim to have wolf anatomy, and their jaws may not be capable of chewing bones thoroughly. Their smaller digestive tracts are more likely to become impacted with bone fragments and their smaller bodies more likely to be severely compromised if they should contract a disease.

Home-Prepared Diets: If you do not want to feed your dog a commercial diet, a far better alternative is to cook homemade meals according to recipes devised by canine nutritionists. Such diets provide a variety of nutrients in fresh foods according to accepted nutritional standards for dogs, but they are more labor intensive than other choices. Do not try to devise such a recipe yourself. Canine nutrition is not the same as human nutrition, and the chances of you cooking up a balanced diet are slim. Ask your veterinarian to suggest a reputable source for home-prepared menus.

Most dogs, unless they've been raised on only one food, prefer a varied menu. Varying a dog's diet can provide some insurance that he is getting proper nutrition by providing a wide range of ingredients. In fact, dogs tend to prefer a novel food but then tire of it within a few days. However, many dogs develop diarrhea at abrupt changes in diet, so you must change foods gradually with these dogs. It is a tribute to the dog's general hardiness that most

Small Talk
Chihuahua Nutrition Needs

Some dog food companies market foods specifically designed for the needs of small dogs. Whether feeding your Chihuahua one of these foods or another, keep these factors in mind:

• Chihuahuas must eat more per pound (per 0.45 kg) than big dogs. For example, a six-pound (2.7 kg) Chihuahua must eat about 47 calories per pound (per 0.45 kg) of body weight in order to maintain weight and condition. In contrast, a 100-pound (45.4 kg) dog would only need 23 calories per pound (per 0.45 kg) of body weight.

• Chihuahuas have small stomachs. This means that you can't just feed your dog a lot of food to make sure he gets enough calories. You may need to feed him more calorie-rich food and more small meals per day.

• Chihuahuas don't eat a lot of food overall, so small snacks can throw off the balance of your dog's diet.

• Chihuahuas, especially very small or very young ones, must eat a little, often, in order to ward off hypoglycemia.

• Chihuahuas should eat foods rich in complex carbohydrates, and avoid simple sugars, to avoid hypoglycemia.

• Chihuahuas need small kibbles so they can crunch up their food rather than have to swallow it whole. Optimally designed kibble doesn't simply break up when chewed but requires the tooth to penetrate it before breaking, adding to its scrubbing action.

• Chihuahuas tend to have dental problems, so if their teeth are in bad shape they may not be able to eat hard food at all, or may require a softer kibble.

• Chihuahuas lose more body heat in cold weather compared to large dogs. Their food should have ample fat content to make up for energy lost in maintaining body heat.

• Chihuahuas tend to be somewhat discriminating in their tastes, even picky. Because they have a reduced olfactory area compared to other breeds, they may not be able to smell and appreciate foods like larger breeds can. It may also be because they live more closely with their owners than do many large dogs, and are used to tasting tidbits from their owners' plates.

---

dogs survive under any of these feeding schemes. But for your Chihuahua to be all that he can be, you may have to do some experimenting and understand some basics of canine nutrition.

Forbidden Foods: A few table scraps won't hurt, as long as they don't cut into your Chi's balanced diet. But choose your scraps carefully. Avoid hunks of fat, which can bring on pancreatitis in susceptible dogs, and avoid the following human foods, which are toxic to dogs.

• Chocolate contains the stimulant theobromine, which can cause shaking, seizures, increased heart rate, and death in dogs. Milk chocolate has about 44 mg of theobromine per ounce (per 28.4 g), semisweet chocolate about 150 mg per ounce (per 28.4 g), and baker's chocolate about 390 mg per ounce (per 28.4 g). About 50 to 100 mg per pound (per 0.45 kg) is considered a lethal dose for dogs. One ounce of baker's chocolate could kill a five-pound (2.3 kg) Chihuahua.

• Coffee in large amounts, and especially coffee beans or grounds, can cause caffeine toxicity in dogs.

• Sugar-free candy and gum containing the artificial sweetener xylitol can cause a potentially fatal drop in blood sugar and lead to liver failure. A five-pound (2.3 kg) Chi that eats as little as a quarter gram of xylitol needs veterinary treatment.

• Onions cause a condition in which the red blood cells are destroyed, in extreme cases leading to anemia and even death. Garlic contains the same ingredient, but in lesser quantity.

• Macadamia nuts cause some dogs to become very ill; the cause isn't understood.

• Raisins and grapes can cause kidney failure and extreme sudden toxicity in some dogs. As little as 0.3 ounces (8.5 g) of grapes per pound (per 0.45 kg) and 0.05 ounces (1.4 g) of raisins per pound (per 0.45 kg) have caused kidney failure in some dogs.

• Yeast bread dough can rise in the gastrointestinal tract, causing obstruction. It also produces alcohol as it rises.

• Alcohol can make dogs drunk just as it does people. It can also kill dogs if they drink too much, which could easily happen with a tiny dog.

• Raw eggs, contrary to popular opinion, are not good for dogs. They prevent the absorption of biotin, an important B vitamin. They can also contain salmonella.

• Apple, apricot, cherry, peach, and plum pits and stems contain a cyanide compound. Signs of toxicity include dilated pupils, difficulty breathing, fast breathing, and shock.

• Nutmeg in large amounts can cause toxicity in dogs. Signs include tremors, seizures, and even death.

• Spoiled food is no safer for dogs than it is for you. It can cause food poisoning, with signs including vomit-

ing, diarrhea, and even death. Moldy food can cause nervous system signs such as tremors.

Evaluating Foods

Dogs are omnivorous, meaning their nutritional needs can best be met by a diet derived from both animals and plants. These nutrients are commercially available in several forms. Dry food (containing about 10 percent moisture) is the most popular, economical, and healthy but least enticing form of dog food. It can be especially difficult for a dog with tooth problems to eat large kibble. Canned foods have a high moisture content (about 75 percent), which helps to make them tasty. However, it also makes them comparatively expensive since you are in essence buying water. Most Chihuahua owners prefer to serve a mixture of dry and canned foods.

If you choose to feed commercial food, feed a high-quality food from a name-brand company that states it meets the recommended minimal nutrient levels for dogs set by the Association of American Feed Control Officials (AAFCO) and has been tested through actual feeding trials. Always strive to buy and use only the freshest food available. Dry food loses nutrients as it sits, and the fat content can become rancid.

Canine Nutrition

When comparing food labels, keep in mind that differences in moisture content can cause difficulties. These differences make comparing the guaranteed analyses in different forms of food difficult to do unless you first do some calculations to equate the percentage of dry matter food. A good rule of thumb is that three or four of the first six ingredients of a dog food should be animal derived. These tend to be tastier and more highly digestible than plant-based ingredients. More highly digestible foods generally mean less stool volume and less gas problems. The components that vary most from one brand to another are protein and fat percentages.

Protein: Protein provides the necessary building blocks for growth and maintenance of bones, muscle, and coat and for the production of infection-fighting antibodies. The quality of protein is as important as its quantity. Meat-derived protein is of higher quality and is more highly digestible than plant-derived protein. This means that two foods with identical protein percentages can differ in the nutritional level of protein according to the protein's source.

Stressed, highly active, or underweight dogs should be fed higher protein levels. Puppies, as well as pregnant and nursing mothers, need particularly high protein levels and somewhat higher fat levels in their diets, such as the levels found in

Small Talk
Semimoist Foods

Semimoist foods (with about 30 percent moisture) contain high levels of sugar used as preservatives. Although they are tasty and convenient, they are not an optimal nutritional choice as a regular diet and especially not suggested as a regular meal for any dog prone to hypoglycemia (see page 127 for more information about hypoglycemia).

puppy foods. Veterinarians used to think that older dogs should be fed low-protein diets in order to avoid kidney problems. However, research has shown that high-protein diets do not cause kidney failure. In fact, high-quality protein is essential to dogs with compromised kidney function. Such dogs should have reduced phosphorous levels, however, and special diets are available that satisfy these requirements. Most adult Chihuahuas will do fine eating regular adult foods that have protein levels of about 20 to 22 percent (dry food percentage).

Fat: Fat is the calorie-rich component of foods, and most dogs prefer the taste of foods with higher fat content. Fat is necessary for good health, aiding in the transport of important vitamins and providing energy. Dogs deficient in fat (usually from diets containing less than 5 percent dry matter fat) may have sparse, dry coats and scaly skin. Excessive fat intake can cause obesity and appetite reduction, creating a deficiency in other nutrients. Obese dogs or dogs with heart problems, pancreatitis, or diarrhea should be fed a low-fat food.

Carbohydrates: The carbohydrates in most dog foods are primarily plant derived. They are a fairly inexpensive source of nutrition and make up a large part of most commercial dog foods. Many carbohydrates are poorly utilized by the dog's digestive system. Those derived from rice are best utilized, those from potato and corn far less so, and wheat, oat, and beans even less again. When these ingredients are cooked, it increases their nutrient availability. Excessive amounts of carbohydrates in the diet can cause decreased performance, diarrhea, and flatulence.

Fiber: Fiber in dog food varies considerably. Better-quality fiber sources include beet pulp and rice bran, but even these should provide just a small percentage of a food's ingredients. Weight-reducing diets often include larger amounts of fiber so the dog will feel fuller and to decrease the digestibility of some of the other nutrients. Too much fiber interferes with digestion and can cause diarrhea or larger stool volume.

A dog's optimal level of each nutrient will change according to his age, energy requirements, and state of health. Prescription commercial diets and recipes for home-prepared diets are available for dogs with various illnesses or needs.

Feeding and Weight

Traditional dog dogma contends that adult dogs should be fed only once a day. This is seldom a good idea for a Chihuahua, however. Many Chihuahuas are prone to hypoglycemia, and the best prevention for this dangerous disorder is eating frequent, small meals. Very young puppies should be fed at least five times a day on a regular schedule. Feed them as much as they care to eat in about 15 minutes. From the age of three to six months, pups should be fed four times daily and fed three times daily until they are about a year old. After that, they should eat twice daily. If you choose to feed more

often, make sure you adjust meal size so that you do not feed your dog too much.

Letting a young Chihuahua self-feed by leaving food available at all times is seldom a good idea. Wet food can spoil and some dogs will overindulge. More importantly, some pups will forget to eat when they should and become hypoglycemic. By feeding the dog discreet meals, you teach the dog to eat when food is offered and you can monitor the dog to make sure he eats properly.

Your dog's weight is the best gauge of whether your dog needs more or less food. All dogs have different metabolisms, so each dog's diet must be adjusted accordingly. The Chihuahua has slender limbs that were not designed to support a heavy body. In a Chihuahua of proper

weight, the ribs should be easily felt through a layer of muscle, but they should not be visible. No roll of fat should be over the withers or rump, but neither the backbone nor the hip bones should be prominent.

Weight-Reducing Diets: Obesity is a major problem in many Chihuahuas. Saying *"No"* to a dog whom you consider such a friend and equal is difficult. Ignoring those big hungry eyes focused on your plate is nearly impossible. Yet only a few morsels constitute a significant extra meal to a Chihuahua, so your small handouts

Small Talk
Water
Water is essential for your dog's health and comfort. Do not just keep your dog's water bowl full by topping it off every day. Such a habit allows algae to form along the sides of the bowl and gives bacteria a chance to multiply. Empty, scrub, and refill the water bowl daily.

can end up making a big difference in your Chihuahua's weight.

Obesity predisposes dogs to joint injuries and heart problems. It also worsens many preexisting problems. Your dog should be checked before embarking on any serious weight-reducing effort. Heart disease and some endocrine disorders, such as hypothyroidism, Cushing's disease, or the early stages of diabetes, can cause the appearance of obesity and should be ruled out or treated. A dog in which only the stomach is enlarged, without fat around the shoulders or rump, is especially suspect and should be examined by a veterinarian.

Chances are your expanding Chihuahua is simply eating more calories than he is expending. If snacks are the problem, put your dog into another room every time you eat or prepare food. Substitute a low-calorie snack alternative such as rice cakes or carrots. Feed your dog a lower-calorie diet. The role of high fiber in reducing diets is controversial; recent studies suggest it does not provide the lowered hunger perception it was

once thought to. Commercially available diet foods supply about 15 percent fewer calories per pound and are preferable to the alternative of just feeding less of a fattening food. Research indicates that protein levels should remain moderate to high in reducing diets in order to avoid the loss of muscle tissue. Home-prepared diets are available that are both tasty and less fattening.

Schedule a walk immediately following your dinner to get your dog's mind off of your leftovers. It will be good for both of you.

Weight-Gaining Diets: A Chihuahua that loses weight rapidly or steadily for no apparent reason should be taken to the veterinarian. Several diseases, including cancer, can cause wasting. A sick or recu-

perating dog may have to be coaxed into eating. Cat food or baby food containing meat are both relished by dogs and may entice a dog without an appetite to eat. Offer cooked chicken breasts or other meat, but ask your veterinarian first. Some prescription drugs may stimulate the appetite slightly.

A few dogs just do not gain weight well, and some are just picky eaters. Underweight dogs may gain weight with puppy food. Add water, milk, bouillon, ground beef, or canned food to the puppy food, and heat slightly to increase the aroma and palatability. Milk will cause many dogs to have diarrhea, so try only a little bit at first. Of course, once you start this, you know you're making your picky eater even pickier!

Ay, Chihuahua
Special Diets

Several diseases can be adversely affected by feeding some normal dog food ingredients; conversely, sometimes the effects of these disorders can be mitigated by diet. Commercial diets are available for most major diseases that are influenced by diet, and home-prepared recipes are also available. Many dogs tire of these diets, however, and owners often supplement with treats that offset the proper nutrition these special diets provide. Understanding the dietary requirements can help you choose proper foods (and treats) for an affected dog. Any restricted diet should be undertaken only under veterinary advice, which is why most commercial diets of this nature are available only through veterinarians.

Congestive Heart Failure

Feeding a low-sodium diet is the foremost dietary requirement for dogs with congestive heart failure. Some dogs also require slightly higher levels of potassium and magnesium. Heart failure also causes a wasting of muscle and often a reduced appetite. This makes keeping adequate weight on these dogs a challenge. Some dogs refuse to eat a low-sodium diet, and sometimes compromises must be made in order for them to eat at all. Look for low-sodium human foods—one example is frosted mini-wheats—that can sometimes be used as treats. Congestive heart failure often brings on kidney failure, which makes finding an appropriate diet that is acceptable to the dog even more challenging.

Chronic Renal Disease

Kidney (renal) disease is one of the more common problems of older dogs. The role of protein in managing chronic renal disease remains controversial, and it varies with the individual dog. Feeding a low-protein diet reduces the work the kidneys must do by reducing toxic waste products from protein. High-quality protein has fewer toxic waste products, so the dog gets the benefits of protein while minimizing its adverse effects. Eggs have the highest-quality protein, followed by milk, and then beef or chicken (with about 75 percent the value of egg protein). Vegetable-derived protein provides even lower-quality protein. A diet containing 8 to 10 percent (dry-matter) high-quality protein is usually good for dogs with renal disease. In addition, the phosphorus intake must be reduced, and the calcium-to-phosphorous levels should be in a 1:1 ratio. Salt should be restricted to control hypertension. The best diet for a Chihuahua with kidney disease must be tailored to that particular dog, based upon veterinary tests and advice. For example, although eggs are an excellent source of protein for most dogs with kidney problems, their high sulfur content makes them a poor choice for dogs that also have marked acidosis—a condition your veterinarian would have to diagnose.

Liver Disease

Dietary management is essential in dogs with liver disease. Of primary importance is that the dog must eat; fasting offers no opportunity for a damaged liver to recover. Meat should be avoided; preferable protein sources include milk, cottage cheese, or tofu. Simple and complex carbohydrates (such as rice, potatoes, and vegetables) are essential and should be fed in small, frequent meals throughout the day. The addition of fat can increase the meal's tastiness. It is essential that Vitamin A be kept to a minimal level, and copper levels must be kept low.

Urinary Stones

Dogs can develop different kinds of urinary stones. The choice of an appropriate diet depends upon the particular kind of stone or, more properly, calculus (either struvite, calcium oxalate, or urate stones/calculi). Struvite calculi are better treated with antibiotic therapy than with dietary management. Calcium oxalate calculi are best prevented with diets low in oxalate and calcium, minimal vitamin D, normal phosphorus levels, and high levels of magnesium and citrate. Urate calculi are best managed with diets low in purines and diets that also encourage increased water consumption.

Diabetes Mellitus

Diabetic dogs should consume a diet high in complex carbohydrates, low in fats, moderate in proteins, and with no simple sugars. Fiber-rich foods tend to be best. The feeding schedule is equally important for these dogs. Designing a successful feeding regime for a diabetic dog will require significant commitment and teamwork with your veterinarian, especially since different diabetic dogs may require different diets.

Food Allergies

Symptoms of food allergies range from diarrhea to itchy skin and ears. If you suspect your dog has a food allergy, consult your veterinarian about an elimination diet, in which you start with a bland diet consisting of ingredients your dog has never eaten before. Lamb and rice foods used to be vigorously promoted as hypoallergenic. However, because a dog is now likely to have eaten lamb previously, that is no longer true. Your veterinarian can suggest sources of protein (such as venison, duck, or rabbit) that your dog will probably not have eaten previously. You may have to keep the dog on this diet for at least a month, withholding treats, pills, and even toys that might be creating an allergic response. If the symptoms go away, then ingredients are added back to the diet gradually, or a novel commercial diet is tried. A lot of experimentation may be necessary, but a healthy and happy dog will be well worth it.

Pancreatitis

Pancreatitis occurs more commonly in older or middle-aged dogs, especially overweight ones. It is often precipitated by a high-fat meal and is the most common illness associated with Thanksgiving and Christmas. Symptoms include lack of appetite, lethargy, signs of abdominal discomfort (such as standing with front legs down on the ground in a bowing position), and possibly vomiting, diarrhea, and even shock or death. Although most dogs can eat a high-fat meal without a problem, once a dog develops pancreatitis, a high-fat meal often precipitates subsequent episodes.

Chapter Six

Good Grooming

One of the appeals of the Chihuahua is the pleasure derived simply from stroking their silken fur, whether they are smooth or long coated. This pleasure is even greater when that fur is clean and healthy. Grooming is not only important for the sake of beauty; it also can prevent serious health problems. Just as with people, good grooming involves more than an occasional brushing of the hair. Keeping the nails, teeth, eyes, and ears well groomed is just as, if not more, important.

Coat Care

The Chihuahua coat is relatively low maintenance. A quick once-over with a soft brush or damp cloth will usually be enough to loosen dirt and impart a good sheen to the hair. Dogs kept indoors under artificial lighting shed year-round, with a major shedding season in the spring. Fortunately, Chihuahuas don't have that much hair to shed! A daily vigorous brushing during shedding season, using a bristle or rubber bristle brush, is the best way to hurry along shedding. More hairs will shed after bathing, and they are especially easy to dislodge when the hair is almost, but not quite yet, dry.

Casual grooming can be done with your dog in your lap or seated beside you on a blanket. However, if you are serious about your results, using a grooming table is helpful. Begin grooming your Chihuahua while he is still a puppy. Use plenty of treats and a small, soft brush. Reward your puppy for standing or lying down calmly. Accustom him to being touched all over. Examine his feet, mouth, and ears. At this point, your Chihuahua's comfort and happiness

in the situation is far more important than your grooming results.

When grooming an adult Long Coat Chihuahua, make sure your brush or comb reaches all the way to the skin. Pay special attention to areas in which tangles are likely to form, such as behind the ears, under the elbows, and in the britches. If you find a mat, don't yank or cut it out. Try to pull it in half lengthwise, and continue to bisect each piece until it can be combed apart. A good rule to keep in mind is to comb the hair out of the mat, not the mat out of the hair. If the process seems impossible, then you can use blunt-nosed scissors to cut the mat out. Wriggle a comb between the mat and the skin so you can't accidentally cut the skin. The shorter hairs that are left from cutting out mats have a greater tendency to mat again, so comb the area every day so another mat doesn't take the first's place.

Bathing and Drying

You can keep your Chihuahua fairly clean without bathing. However, snuggling with him will be nicer if he is bathed occasionally. Between baths you can bathe him with a rinse-free shampoo. These shampoos are applied to the coat, which is then simply rubbed dry. You can also apply cornstarch to help fluff and clean a coat. For the best results, however, nothing takes the place of a real bath.

Shampoo Selection: Since you're bathing such a little dog, you can afford to splurge on the best dog shampoo available. Even the fanciest

human shampoos do not work on dogs as well as these. Since dog hair and human hair have different pH values, they need different shampoos. Dog skin has a pH of 7.5, while human skin has a pH of 5.5. Bathing in a shampoo formulated for the pH of human skin can lead to scaling and irritation. If, however, your dog has a healthy coat and you just want a simple bath, using a human shampoo is fine.

Some shampoos have whiteners, and some have ingredients that claim to bring out the colors (the latter have very little, if any, such effect). Other shampoos are available from your veterinarian and are effective for various skin problems. Oatmeal-based antipruritics can help soothe itchy skin. Moisturizing shampoos can help with dry skin. Antiseborrheic sham-

poos can help with excessive grease, scaling, and dandruff. Antimicrobials can help with damaged skin.

Bathing: The easiest place to wash your Chihuahua is in a sink with a handheld sprayer. You can place a nonslip rubber pad into the bottom so your dog will feel more comfortable. Chihuahuas get cold easily. Warm the room beforehand, and use warm water. Warm water also tends to open the hair follicles and helps loosen dead hair. Keep one hand under the spray so you can monitor the water temperature.

Start by wetting down the dog to the skin, leaving the head for last. Be sure the water isn't just running off the top of the dog. You need to soak the undercoat down to the skin. Mix the shampoo with water first. Work up a moderate lather. Do not let water get into the ears or shampoo into the eyes. Rinsing is a crucial step; shampoo remaining in the coat can cause dryness and itchiness. Begin rinsing from the front and top of the dog, and work backward and rearward. Then follow with a cream rinse.

Drying: Have a towel ready for initial drying. Don't let your dog outside on a chilly day when he is still damp from a bath. You have removed the oils from the coat and saturated your dog down to the skin. Using a handheld blow-dryer is ideal for finishing the drying. Again, hold your hand in front of the blown air so you will recognize when it is too warm for the dog's comfort. Too intense heat can damage the coat and even burn the skin.

The Long Coat Chihuahua should not have hair that puffs out, but sometimes blow-drying tends to make the coat puffier. This isn't a problem unless you are getting ready for a show, in which case you need to take care to blow and brush the coat only in the direction of its growth. This will reduce any tendency for crimps or waves to form and also helps the fur lie closer to the body.

The hair of some Long Coat Chihuahuas may tend to stand off the body too much; these dogs are better off not being blow-dried if you want their coats to lie flatter. They should instead be partially dried, then brushed in the direction of hair growth, and then placed into something that will hold the hair down for the final drying. The simplest solution is to take a section of a nylon stocking about the same length as the dog's body and cut small holes for the dog's legs and neck (and for males, the penis). Have your dog wear this nylon sweater for several hours before removing it, and then again brush the hair in the direction of growth. You should not let your dog play or run about unsupervised when wearing the stocking. In addition, because drying time is slowed by wearing it, you must take care that the dog does not get chilled during the process.

Trimming

Very little, or no, trimming is required for dogs that are not destined for the showring. Even in the showring, very little trimming is required or even desired. Errant hairs can be snipped off, but a sculpted look is not desirable. Some people trim the vibrissae (whiskers) off of show dogs. However, unless they are particularly distracting or unsightly, leaving them on is preferable. The vibrissae are actually important sensory organs that many people believe help the dog avoid damage to the eyes and face. Trimming them is still a matter of personal preference, however.

The amount of trimming required to make a Smooth Coat look his best for the ring varies according to the type of coat the dog has. Some Smooths tend to grow especially thick coats around the neck and ruff area, giving the illusion that the dog

has a short, thick neck. Others have a slightly thicker coat than desirable all over their body, causing them to appear overly bulky. You can sometimes thin these coats by running a stripping comb over them to remove some of the undercoat. You can also neaten up the scraggly hairs that tend to form around the backs of the thighs and under the belly. Most exhibitors do carefully trim long hairs from between the pads under the feet and also any hairs that extend beyond the nails.

Long Coats don't require much trimming, either. The hair between the pads is trimmed. Any hair that extends so far beyond the nails that it gives the appearance of the dog wearing slippers, or worse, snowshoes, is trimmed. The correct shape of the foot is midway between a round cat foot and a long hare foot. Improper trimming can give the illusion of a foot that is either too round or too long, and proper trimming can make a poor foot look better than it really is. Thinning shears can be used to give the foot a more natural appearance.

The long hair on the inner surface of the ear may be trimmed so that the size of the ear can be better appreciated. Sometimes the britches will be so full that they will give the illusion of an overly long body. In such cases, they may be thinned (using thinning shears) slightly. No matter where you thin or trim, the hair should look untouched. Hair should never appear sculpted but, rather, should have a somewhat wispy, natural look. When in doubt, leaving too much on rather than taking too much off is always preferable.

Skin Problems

Grooming gives you the chance to examine the condition of the skin. Skin problems can be uncomfortable and unsightly, and they often lead to hair loss. Problems can result from parasites, allergies, bacteria, fungi, endocrine disorders, and a long list of other possible causes.

Skin Allergies: Flea allergy dermatitis (FAD) is the most common of all skin problems. When even one flea bites a susceptible dog, the flea's saliva causes an allergic reaction that results in intense itching. This occurs not only in the vicinity of the flea bite but often all over the dog and especially on his rump, legs, and paws. The dog chews these areas and causes irritation, leading to crusted bumps.

Besides FAD, dogs can have allergic reactions to pollens or other inhaled allergens. Whereas human inhalant allergies usually result in respiratory symptoms, canine inhalant allergies usually result in itchy skin. The condition typically first appears in young dogs and gets progressively worse. The main sites of itching seem to be the face, ears, feet, forelegs, armpits, and abdomen. The dog rubs and chews these areas, traumatizing the skin and leading to secondary bacterial infections. Because the feet are so often affected, many people erroneously assume the dog is allergic to grass or dew. Although such contact allergies do exist, they occur far less commonly than flea, inhalant, or food allergies.

Dogs can also have food allergies that can cause itching. They are discussed on page 69.

Allergens can be isolated with an intradermal skin test, in which small amounts of various allergen extracts are injected under the skin. The skin is then monitored for localized allergic

Small Talk
Color Dilution Alopecia

Dogs of several breeds, including Chihuahuas, can come in an eye-catching gray or blue color. This color is the result of the pairing of two recessive genes for dilution that cause hair that would normally be black to be gray instead. For some reason, these gray hairs are often associated with skin problems. The gray hair may be lost gradually, starting along the top of the neck and extending along the back line. The gray hair itself may be brittle, and the skin beneath it may be prone to staphylococcal infections. These problems may start while a puppy. Not all blue Chihuahuas are affected equally. Interestingly, those that are lighter shades of gray are more likely to be affected, as are those having two blue parents. No cure is available. The best you can do is to feed a healthy diet and keep a close watch for infections.

reactions. Blood tests are also available and are less expensive, but they are not as comprehensive as skin testing. Either test should be performed by a veterinarian with training in the field of allergic skin diseases since the results can be difficult to interpret.

External Parasites

Parasites remain one of the most common causes of skin and coat problems in dogs. Their damage is more than skin deep, however. Many external parasites also carry serious, even deadly, systemic diseases.

Fleas: Fleas have long been the bane of dogs, but recent advances have finally put dog owners onto the winning side in the fight against fleas. In any but the mildest of infestations, the new products available are well worth their initial higher purchase price. Putting an expensive product onto your dog once every three months is a lot cheaper than reapplying a cheap one every day.

Always read the ingredients. You may think you're getting a deal with a less-expensive product that is applied the same and boasts of the same results as one of the more expensive products, but you're not getting a deal if it doesn't contain the right ingredients. Some of the major ingredients in the most popular of these products include the following.

• Imidacloprid (for example, Advantage) is a liquid applied once a month on the animal's back. It gradually distributes itself over the entire skin surface. It kills at least 98 percent of the fleas on the animal within 24 hours and will continue to kill fleas for a month. It can withstand water but not repeated swimming or bathing.

• Fipronil (for example, Frontline) comes as either a spray that you apply all over the dog's body or as a self-distributing liquid applied only on the dog's back (the spray is usually more economical for a small Chihuahua). Once applied, fipronil collects in the hair follicles and then wicks out over time. Thus, it is resistant to being washed off and can kill fleas for up to three months on dogs. It is also effective on ticks for a shorter period.

• Spinosad (for example, Comfortis) is a chewable tablet that starts killing fleas within 30 minutes and lasts for a month. It has no effect on ticks. It is

---

Small Talk
Tapeworms and Fleas

Tapeworms look like moving, white, flat worms when fresh or like rice grains (usually around the dog's anus) when dried out. Although they are one of the least debilitating of all the worms, their segments can produce anal itching. Because tapeworms are in the cestode family, they are not affected by the same kinds of dewormers and preventives as the other common worms, which are in the nematode family. The only preventive is to rid your Chihuahua of fleas diligently because fleas transmit the most common tapeworm (*Dipylidium*) to dogs.

only for dogs weighing more than 5 pounds.

• Dinototefuran (for example, Vectra) is applied on the dog's back and is effective against four types of ticks, three types of mosquitoes, and all fleas.

• Selamectin is a self-distributing liquid that kills fleas for one month. It also kills ear mites and several internal parasites, and acts as a heartworm preventive.

• Nitenpyram (for example, Capstar) is an oral medication that starts killing fleas in 20 minutes; all fleas are killed in four hours. It has almost no residual activity, so it's best used as a quick fix for heavily infested dogs.

• Lufenuron, methoprene, or fenoxycarb are chemicals that interfere with the hatching of flea eggs.

Traditional flea-control products are either less effective or less safe than these newer products. The permethrins and pyrethrins are safe but have virtually no residual action. The large family of cholinesterase inhibitors last a little longer but have been known to kill dogs when overused, when used in combination with cholinesterase-inhibiting yard products, or when used with cholinesterase-inhibiting dewormers. Loading the environment with pesticides is an especially unwise choice with tiny dogs that live so close to the ground.

Ultrasonic flea-repelling collars have been shown to be both ineffective on fleas and irritating to dogs. Feeding dogs brewer's yeast or garlic will not get rid of fleas.

Ticks: Two products for tick control are amitraz collars (tick collars) and fipronil spray or liquid. Neither will keep ticks totally off your dog, but they may discourage ticks from staying or implanting. Even with these precautions, you should still use your hands to feel for ticks on your dog whenever you are in a potentially tick-infested area.

Ticks can be found anywhere on the dog but most often burrow around the ears, neck, chest, and between the toes. To remove a tick, use a tissue or tweezers since some

Small Talk
Ehrlichiosis and Ticks

Ehrlichiosis is an underdiagnosed yet potentially fatal disease spread by ticks that parasitizes white blood cells and cripples the immune system. Symptoms may include lack of energy, dullness of coat, occasional vomiting, occasional loss of appetite, coughing, arthritis, muscle wasting, seizures, spontaneous bleeding, anemia, or a host of other nonspecific signs. Aside from a fever in the initial phases of the disease, dogs may not exhibit definite signs of illness—they may just not seem quite right. Definitive diagnosis is made by getting a blood titer and testing for all strains of *Ehrlichia*. The disease can be treated effectively if caught early.

diseases can be transmitted to humans. Grasp the tick as close to the skin as possible, and pull slowly and steadily, trying not to leave the head in the dog. Do not squeeze the tick since this can inject its contents into the dog. Clean the site with alcohol. Often a bump will remain after the tick is removed, even if you got the head. It will go away with time.

Mites: Mites are tiny organisms that are in the tick and spider family. Chemicals that are effective on fleas have no effect on mites. Of the many types of mites, only a few typically cause problems in dogs.

Sarcoptes mites cause sarcoptic mange. This causes intense itching, often characterized by scaling of the ear tips and small bumps and crusts on other affected areas. Most of the lesions are found on the ear tips, abdomen, elbows, and hocks. Treatment requires repeated shampoos or dips of not only the affected dog but other household pets that are in contact with the infected dog. Sarcoptic mange is highly contagious, even to humans, and spread by direct contact. Skin scrapings may reveal the responsible *Sarcoptes scabiei* mite. The presence of just one mite lends a definite diagnosis, but the absence of mites does not mean they aren't present.

Demodex mites cause demodectic mange. Unlike sarcoptic mange, it is not contagious and is not usually itchy. Most cases of demodectic mange appear in puppies, and most consist of only a few patches that often go away by themselves. This

localized variety is not considered hereditary. In some cases, it begins as a diffuse, moth-eaten appearance, particularly around the lips and eyes or on the front legs, or the dog may have many localized spots. These cases tend to get worse until the dog has generalized demodectic mange. Demodectic mange affecting the feet is also common and can be extremely resistant to treatment. A definite diagnosis with a skin scraping should be performed before beginning treatment and before ending it. Because the *Demodex canis* mite is thought to be a normal inhabitant of the dog's hair follicles, the presence of an occasional mite is not normally sufficient evidence to diagnose a dog with demodectic mange.

Cheyletiella mites are contagious and cause mild itchiness. They look like small white specks in the dog's hair near the skin. Many flea insecticides also kill these mites, but they are better treated by using special shampoos or dips.

Sarcoptes, Demodex, and *Cheyletiella* mites have all been successfully eradicated with ivermectin therapy. This treatment is considered off label and should be performed only by a veterinarian in serious cases.

Ear Mites: A dog with ear mites will scratch his ears, shake his head, and perhaps hold his head sideways. The ear mite's signature is a dark, dry, waxy build-up resembling coffee grounds in the ear canal, usually of both ears. Sometimes the tiny mites can be seen with a magnifying glass if the material is placed onto a dark background.

Separate a dog with ear mites from other pets, and wash your hands after handling his ears. Ideally, every pet in a household should be

treated. Your veterinarian can provide the best medication. Because ear mites are also found in the dog's fur all over his body, you should also treat the dog's fur with a pyrethrin-based shampoo or spray.

Ear Care

Unlike in humans, the dog's ear canal is made up of an initially long vertical segment that then abruptly angles to run horizontally toward the skull. This configuration provides a moist environment in which various ear infections can flourish. Fortunately, the Chihuahua's pricked ears allow for good air flow, and ear problems do not commonly occur in the breed.

Ear problems can be difficult to cure once they have become established, so early veterinary attention is crucial. Signs of ear problems include inflammation, discharge, debris, foul odor, pain, scratching, shaking, tilting of the head, or circling to one side. Bacterial and yeast infections, ear mites or ticks, foreign bodies, inhalant allergies, seborrhea, or hypothyroidism are possible underlying problems. Because the ear canal is lined with skin, any skin disorder that affects the dog elsewhere can also strike the ears. Grass awns (or seeds) are a common cause of ear problems in dogs that spend time outdoors. Keep the ear lubricated with mineral oil, and seek veterinary treatment as soon as possible.

If your dog has ear debris but no signs of discomfort or itching, you

Chihuahuas are born with floppy ears that only gradually begin to stand erect as they age. The age at which they stand varies, but most pups have ears that stand by three to four months of age. Not uncommonly, previously standing ears sometimes flop back over during teething, but such ears usually stand back up on their own after teething is finished. Some dogs need a little help, however. Breeders use various methods for training the ears to stand, including taping them up and together in a similar fashion as that used in training cropped ears to stand erect. You can also shave the inside of the ear and use something like toupee glue or false eyelash glue to adhere a soft moleskin or foam form inside the ear to keep it erect. Anything you put onto the ears should be removed every two or three days for a day or so. Usually the problem will be cured after a week or two of taping. If the pup reaches six months of age and has never had ears that would stand, chances are against them ever standing.

can try cleaning the ear yourself. Be forewarned that overzealous cleaning can irritate the skin lining the ear canal. You can buy products to clean the ear or use a homemade mixture of one part alcohol to two parts white vinegar. First, make sure you are outdoors. Hold the ear near its base, and quickly squeeze in the ear cleaner (the slower it drips, the more it will tickle). Gently massage the liquid downward, and squish it all around. Then stand back and let your dog shake it all out (which is usually why you want to be outdoors). If the ear has so much debris that repeated rinses don't clean it right up, you have a problem that will need veterinary attention. If the ear is red, swollen, or painful, do not attempt to clean it yourself. Your dog may need to be sedated for cleaning and may have a serious problem. Cleaning solutions will flush debris but will not kill mites or cure infections. Do not stick cotton swabs down into the ear canal since they can irritate the skin and pack debris into the horizontal canal. Do not use powders in the ear, which can cake, or hydrogen peroxide, which can leave the ear moist.

Eye Care

Eye care should never be approached with a wait-and-see attitude. Take note of squinting, redness, itching, tearing, dullness, mucus discharge, or any change in pupil size or reactivity. Any time your dog's pupils do not react to light or when one eye reacts differently from another, take him to the veterinarian immediately. This could indicate a serious ocular or neurological problem.

A thick mucus discharge usually indicates a problem that requires veterinary attention. A clear watery discharge can be a symptom of a foreign body, allergies, or a tear drainage problem. A clogged tear drainage duct can cause the tears to drain onto the face rather than through the nose as normal. Your veterinarian can diagnose a drainage problem with a simple test. Some very small dogs simply have tear ducts that are too small to drain away all the tears. The best you can do is to keep the face of such a dog as clean and tear free as possible.

Small Talk
Tear Stains

In some Chihuahuas, excessive tearing from the eyes causes reddish stains on the fur of the face. This is an indication that you need to get a veterinarian to look for the cause. In some dogs, no obvious cause can be found and no treatment is available. Washing the tears from the face several times a day can help prevent the stains, as can coating the area with petroleum jelly (Vaseline). You can also place a drop of sterile eye wash into the eyes once a day. It seems to dilute the tears on the skin and helps minimize staining. It also helps to wash out any debris that could be irritating the eye. To remove the stain, mix about equal parts of hydrogen peroxide and milk of magnesia with enough cornstarch to form a thick paste. Carefully swab it onto the stain and allow it to dry, then brush the mixture off. This will remove the stain, but it will also bleach dark hair.

Nail Care

All canine nails evolved to withstand strenuous running and digging. Even though your Chihuahua may run amok throughout your home, chances are you are going to need to help keep his nails trimmed. This is especially true for older or more sedate dogs. The most common problem associated with overly long nails happens when the nail becomes snagged on something like a carpet loop, pulling the nail from its bed or dislocating the toe. In addition, overly long nails impact on the ground with every step, causing discomfort and eventually splayed feet and lameness. If dew claws (the rudimentary thumbs on the wrists) are left untrimmed, they can get caught on things even more easily and can be ripped out. Alternatively they can actually loop around and grow into the dog's leg. You must prevent this by trimming your dog's nails every week or two.

Cutting the nails with the dog lying on his back in your lap is easiest. If your dog will not tolerate this, you can also try to have a helper hold him while you cut the nails, holding the feet backward much as a horse's hoof is held when being shod. This way your dog can't see what's going on, which can often help him remain calm.

Use a small nail trimmer; even those for cats work well. Be sure to cut off just the hooklike end. When viewed from beneath the nail, you will see a solid core culminating in a hollowed nail. Cut the tip up to the core but not beyond. On occasion,

you will slip up and cause the nail to bleed. Apply styptic powder to the nail to stop the bleeding. If this is not available, dip the nail into flour or hold it to a wet tea bag, and be more careful next time! Always end a nail-trimming session with a treat.

Dental Care

Correct occlusion (commonly called *bite*) is important for good dental health. In a correct Chihuahua bite, the top incisors should fit snugly in front of the bottom incisors, with the top canines just behind the bottom canines. If the bottom canines are behind or opposed to the top canines, the bottom ones can be displaced inward and pierce the palate.

Small dogs tend to have problems with crowded teeth, which can some-times displace teeth and affect the occlusion. Between four and seven months of age, Chihuahua puppies will begin to shed their baby teeth and show off new permanent teeth. Often deciduous (baby) teeth, especially the canines (fangs), are not shed, so that the permanent teeth grow in beside the baby teeth. If this condition persists after the permanent teeth are fully in, consult your veterinarian. Retained baby teeth can cause misalignment of adult teeth. Some veterinarians advocate removing any deciduous teeth as soon as they seem to be interfering.

A dog's jaws grow somewhat independently of each other. Therefore, one of the factors that results in the jaws growing to the same approximate length and at the same approximate rate is the interlock of the teeth. This dental interlock will actually pull or push the teeth of the opposing jaw and prevent one jaw from growing past the other. This works well in most cases. However, if the jaws do get out of correct position, the teeth can actually prevent them from getting realigned. If the jaws are incorrectly positioned, removing some deciduous teeth may help the occlusion improve. Removing teeth only after taking radiographs (X-rays) is a good idea so the veterinarian can make sure permanent teeth are below the gumline to take their place. Some toy dogs never develop permanent teeth, and when their deciduous teeth are removed, they are left with only gums showing! Also, be extremely careful that your

The problem starts with plaque, which leads to tartar, gingivitis, gum recession, and tooth loss.

If you let plaque build up, it attracts bacteria and minerals, which harden into tartar. The plaque spreads rootward, causing irreversible periodontal disease with tissue, bone, and tooth loss. The bacteria gain an inlet to the bloodstream, where they can cause kidney and heart valve infections.

Being vigilant about dental care is the best way to save your dog's teeth. Dental care begins in puppyhood, as you teach your Chi to enjoy getting his teeth brushed. You can use a soft-bristle toothbrush and meat-flavored doggy toothpaste. Use a dog toothpaste; remember, dogs don't rinse and spit! Make it a habit to brush once a day.

veterinarian recognizes which teeth are to be removed. Adult Chihuahua teeth are so tiny that they are easily mistaken for deciduous teeth. More than one distraught Chihuahua breeder has discovered their veterinarian had accidentally removed permanent teeth.

Like most small dogs, Chihuahuas have a high incidence of dental disease. In fact, according to one study, tooth and gum problems are the most common reason for consulting a veterinarian among owners of Chihuahuas between the ages of 4 and 10 years. Small breeds have comparatively less jawbone density to support their teeth compared to large breeds, and their teeth are comparatively large for their mouths, resulting in crowded teeth with somewhat shallow roots. Many Chis start losing their adult teeth at a very early age.

Hard, crunchy foods can help, but they won't take the place of brushing. However, special foods are available from your veterinarian that are designed to scrape against the dog's teeth. They allow the tooth to penetrate deep inside the kibble before the kibble breaks, and the kibble also has abrasive properties that scour the tooth surface. These foods may not work miracles, but they are helpful, especially for dogs who will not allow you to brush their teeth. If tartar accumulates, your Chi may need a thorough cleaning under anesthesia.

A well-groomed Chihuahua feels better, looks better, and has a head start on a long and healthy life. You wouldn't want any less for the Chihuahua you love.

Chapter Seven

For the Health of Your Chihuahua

Most breeds that are extremely popular are beset with health problems. This is not the case with Chihuahuas. Even Chihuahuas can get sick, however, and some illnesses that would be minor in larger dogs can be major in these tiny dogs. This makes your job as health guardian all that more crucial. Knowing the difference between normal and abnormal can help you catch a problem before it becomes all too apparent.

Signs of a Healthy Chihuahua

Understanding the normal values for your dog will help you detect when something is not right. The following describes four signs you can monitor.

Gum Color: The simplest yet most overlooked checkpoint is your dog's gum color. Looking at the gums is so simple, yet virtually no one does it—except your veterinarian, who will often look at the gums before anything else when your dog comes into the exam room sick.

• Normal gum color is a good deep pink.
• Pale gum color can indicate anemia or poor circulation.
• White or very light gum color can indicate shock, severe anemia, or very poor circulation.
• Bluish gum or tongue color indicates an imminent, life-threatening lack of oxygen.
• Bright-red gum color can indicate carbon monoxide poisoning.
• Yellowish color can indicate jaundice.
• Little tiny red splotches (called petechia) can indicate a blood-clotting problem.

Do not confuse a red line around the gum line with healthy gums. A dog with dirty teeth can have gum disease, giving an unhealthy, but rosy, glow to the gums, especially at the margins around the teeth.

Besides color, capillary refill time, which is an index of blood circulation, can be estimated simply by pressing on the gum with your finger and lifting

your finger off. The gum where you pressed will be white momentarily but will quickly repink as the blood moves back into the area. If repinking takes longer than a couple of seconds, circulation is poor.

Body Temperature: Your Chihuahua's body temperature is another clue about what's going on inside. As in humans, temperature will be slightly lower in the morning and higher in the evening. Normal temperature for a Chihuahua is about 101°F to 102°F (38.3°C to 38.9°C). If the temperature is:

• 103°F (39.4°C) or above, call the veterinarian and ask for advice.

• 105°F (40.6°C) or above, go to the veterinarian. A temperature of 106°F (41.1°C) and above is dangerous.

• 98°F (36.7°C) or below, call the veterinarian and ask for advice. Meanwhile, treat the dog for hypothermia (see page 106).

• 96°F (35.6°C) or below, go to the veterinarian. Treat for hypothermia on the way.

Pulse: The easiest way to check your dog's pulse is to feel the pulse through the femoral artery. If your dog is standing, cup your hand around the top of his hind leg and feel around the inside of the leg, almost where the leg joins with the torso. If your dog is on his back, you may even see the pulse in this area. Normal pulse rate for a Chihuahua at rest is about 70 to 120 beats per minute.

You can feel your dog's heartbeat by placing your hand onto his lower

Ay, Chihuahua!
Blood Tests

Your Chihuahua's blood can provide valuable clues about the animal's health. Blood tests are vital before your dog undergoes surgery to ensure that he's healthy enough for the procedure. The most common tests are the complete blood count (CBC) and the serum chemistry profile (chem panel). Many other specialized tests are used fairly commonly. Note that abbreviations used by different labs may vary.

The CBC report includes information about:
• Red blood cells: the cells responsible for carrying oxygen throughout the body.
• White blood cells: the infection-fighting cells.
• Platelets: the components responsible for clotting blood in order to stop bleeding.

The chem panel includes information about:
• Albumin (ALB): reduced levels are suggestive of liver or kidney disease or of parasites.

• Alanine aminotransferase (ALT): elevated levels suggest liver disease.
• Alkaline phosphatase (ALKP): elevated levels can indicate liver disease or Cushing's syndrome.
• Amylase (AMYL): elevated levels suggest pancreatic or kidney disease.
• Blood urea nitrogen (BUN): elevated levels suggest kidney disease.
• Calcium (CA): elevated levels suggest kidney or parathyroid disease or some types of tumors.
• Cholesterol (CHOL): elevated levels suggest liver or kidney disease, or several other disorders.
• Creatinine (CREA): elevated levels suggest kidney disease or urinary obstruction.
• Blood glucose (GLU): low levels can suggest liver disease.
• Phosphorous (PHOS): elevated levels can suggest kidney disease.
• Total bilirubin (TBIL): abnormal level can indicate problems in the bile ducts.
• Total protein (TP): abnormal level can indicate problems of the liver, kidney, or gastrointestinal tract.

rib cage just behind his elbow. Do not be alarmed if it seems irregular; the heartbeat of many dogs is irregular compared with that of humans. Have your veterinarian check it out, then get used to how the heartbeat feels when normal.

Hydration: Repeated vomiting, diarrhea, or overheating can quickly lead to dehydration. To check your dog's hydration, pick up the skin on the back just above the shoulders so that it makes a slight tent above the body. The skin should pop back into place almost immediately. If it remains tented and separated from the body, your dog is dehydrated. The most obvious treatment is to give your dog some water. In severe cases or in cases in which the dog cannot eat or drink, your veterinarian may need to give the dog fluids intravenously.

The Five-Minute Checkup

The best five minutes you can spend with your dog every week is performing a quick health check. You will get to know how your dog looks when he's healthy, and you will get a head start treating any problems. As a benefit, your dog will think you just cannot resist petting him all over. Check the following:

• Mouth for red, bleeding, swollen, or pale gums; loose teeth; ulcers of the tongue or gums; or bad breath.

• Eyes for discharge, cloudiness, or discolored whites.

• Ears for foul odor, redness, discharge, or crusted tips.

• Nose for thickened or colored discharge.

• Skin for parasites, hair loss, crusts, red spots, or lumps.

• Feet for cuts, abrasions, split nails, bumps, or misaligned toes.

• Anal region for redness, swelling, discharge, or tracts.

Watch your dog for signs of lameness or incoordination, sore neck, circling, loss of muscle, and any behavioral change. Run your hands over the muscles and bones, and

Most veterinarians advocate neutering and spaying dogs that will not be used for breeding. Not only do these procedures negate the chance of accidental litters, but they also do away with the headaches of dealing with a dog in season. In addition, some health benefits are associated with these procedures.

Spaying (surgical removal of ovaries and uterus) before the first season drastically reduces the chances of breast or uterine cancer as well as pyometra. Tumors of the mammary glands are among the most common of cancers in the dog, occurring mostly in females that were not spayed early in life. Spaying after the age of two years does not impart the protection against mammary cancer that earlier spaying does. Approximately 50 percent of all mammary tumors are malignant.

Castration (neutering) is the surgical removal of the testicles. It eliminates the chance of the dog developing testicular cancer.

check that they are symmetrical from one side to the other. Weigh your dog, and observe whether he is gaining or losing. Check for any growths, swellings, sores, or pigmented lumps. Look out for mammary masses, changes in testicle size, discharge from the vulva or penis, increased or decreased urination, foul smelling or strangely colored urine, incontinence, swollen abdomen, black or bloody stools, changes in appetite or water consumption, difficulty breathing, lethargy, coughing, gagging, or loss of balance. Remember always to be on the alert for signs of hypoglycemia (page 127), especially in puppies, in tiny dogs, or during stressful times.

Behavioral Changes

When a normally active, impetuous Chihuahua suddenly slows down for no apparent reason, it's worth investigating. Lethargy is the most common behavioral sign of disease. Possible causes could include:

• Infection (check for fever).
• Anemia (check gum color).
• Circulatory problem (check gum color and pulse).
• Pain (check limbs, neck, and vertebrae for signs of discomfort upon movement; check mouth, ears, and eyes for signs of pain; check abdomen for pain—pain in the abdomen often causes dogs to stand in a hunched position).
• Sudden loss of vision.
• Poisoning (check gum color, pupil reaction—they should get smaller when a bright light is shined onto them, and look for signs of vomiting or abdominal pain).
• Cancer.
• Metabolic diseases.
• Hypoglycemia (see page 127).

Unprecedented behavior of any kind, but particularly persistent circling or pacing, disorientation, loss of balance, head pressing, hiding, tremors, seizures, lack of bowel or urine control, or a dramatic change in appetite are usually signs of a physical

Ay, Chihuahua!
Tracheal Collapse

The trachea is the windpipe through which your dog breathes. It is actually a flexible tube made up of a series of cartilaginous rings connected by soft tissue. In some dogs, the cartilage in the rings undergoes changes (technically, it has a reduced amount of glycoprotein and glycosaminoglycan) that reduce the ability of the cartilage to retain water, resulting in lowered rigidity. These cartilage abnormalities are probably present at birth. Many dogs with abnormal cartilage can live many years, or even their entire lives, without the condition progressing to tracheal collapse. Other factors usually seem necessary to produce symptoms of tracheal collapse. These factors include obesity, inhalation of irritants or allergens, respiratory infection, enlarged heart, and endotracheal intubation. However, the exact manner in which they bring on tracheal collapse is not documented. The rings collapse such that the top of the trachea flattens, obstructing the airway. This may occur near the part of the trachea closest to the head (cervical region), nearest the lungs (thoracic region), or both. If the collapse occurs in the cervical region, problems tend to arise when the dog breathes in. If the collapse occurs in the thoracic region, problems are more likely when the dog breathes out or coughs.

When the airway is blocked, the dog coughs in a reflexive attempt to open it. Coughing tends to irritate and weaken the trachea further, ultimately causing the condition to worsen.

When tracheal collapse is seen, it is almost always in middle-aged or older Chihuahuas. It rarely occurs in young Chihuahuas, since time is needed for the condition to deteriorate to the point that the owner suspects a problem.

Coughing is the major symptom. The cough is described as a dry, harsh goose honk type of sound. It occurs mostly during the day and is associated with excitement, pressure to the throat, or eating and drinking. In severe cases,

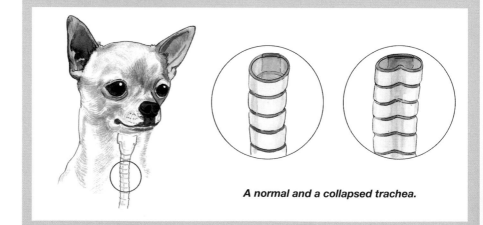

A normal and a collapsed trachea.

the dog may show symptoms of lack of oxygen, including fainting and a bluish tinge to the gums. Radiographs and ultrasound can be used to make an initial diagnosis. The best diagnostic procedure is a tracheoscopy, which actually allows the veterinarian to see the problem areas from within the trachea.

Treatment is usually aimed at controlling the symptoms. Weight reduction of obese dogs is essential since it can bring about very rewarding improvements. Collars should never be used. Harnesses are a better alternative. However, even then care must be taken to avoid putting any pressure onto the dog's throat. Humidifying the air, especially in dry climates, is beneficial. The environment should be kept free of inhaled irritants, especially cigarette smoke. Dogs should not be taken to places where they would be exposed to respiratory diseases; any such infection should be treated immediately. Cough suppressants should be used to reduce irritation to the trachea. The use of bronchodilators may be recommended but is somewhat controversial. Glucosamine and vitamin C supplementation has been suggested to help strengthen cartilage.

In severe cases, surgery may be the only option. Unfortunately, it is not always successful. Surgery is somewhat more rewarding in cases in which the cervical region is the problem and in younger dogs. The most successful method at present is the use of prosthetic supports external to the trachea. Researchers are still working to develop better procedures. Therefore, if you are contemplating surgery for your dog, you need to consult with a veterinary surgeon who is abreast of the very latest developments in this field and who has experience with these surgeries.

problem. They need to be checked by your veterinarian.

Diarrhea

Diarrhea can result from overexcitement or nervousness, a change in diet or water, sensitivity to certain foods, overeating, intestinal parasites, viral or bacterial infections, or ingestion of toxic substances. Bloody diarrhea, diarrhea with vomiting, fever, or other signs of toxicity or a diarrhea that lasts for more than a day should not be allowed to continue without veterinary advice. Some of these could be symptomatic of potentially fatal disorders. In addition, diarrhea can precipitate hypoglycemia.

Less-severe diarrhea can be treated at home by withholding or severely restricting food and water for 24 hours. Because of the threat of hypoglycemia, especially in puppies, do not withhold food entirely. Ice cubes can be given to satisfy thirst. Administer human antidiarrhea medication in the same weight dosage as recommended for humans. A bland diet consisting of rice, tapioca, or cooked macaroni, along with cottage cheese or tofu for protein, should be given for several days. The intestinal tract needs time off in order to heal.

Vomiting

Vomiting is a common occurrence that may or may not indicate a serious problem. Vomiting after eating grass often occurs and is usually of no great concern. Overeating is a common cause of occasional vomiting in puppies, especially if they follow eating with playing. Feed smaller meals more frequently if this becomes a problem. Vomiting immediately after meals could indicate an obstruction of the esophagus. Repeated vomiting could indicate that the dog has eaten spoiled food, undigestible objects, or may have a stomach illness. Veterinary advice should be sought. Meanwhile, withhold food (or feed as directed for diarrhea) and restrict water.

Consult your veterinarian immediately if your dog vomits a foul substance resembling fecal matter (indicating a blockage in the intestinal tract) or blood (partially digested blood resembles coffee grounds) or if there is projectile or continued vomiting. Sporadic vomiting with poor appetite and generally poor condition could indicate internal parasites or a more serious internal disease that should also be checked by your veterinarian.

Coughing

Allergies, foreign bodies, pneumonia, parasites, tracheal collapse, tumors, kennel cough, and heart disease can all cause coughing. Any persistent cough should be checked by your veterinarian. Coughing irritates the throat and can lead to secondary infections (and in some dogs, tracheal collapse) if allowed to continue unchecked. It can also be miserable for the dog.

Kennel Cough is a highly communicable airborne disease caused by several different infectious agents (but most often by *Bordetella*). It is characterized by a gagging cough arising about a week after exposure. Inoculations are available and are an especially good idea if you plan to have your dog around other dogs at training classes or while being boarded.

Heart Disease (specifically, congestive heart failure) can result in coughing, most often following exercise or in the evening. The cough is usually characterized as a moist cough, often ending in a retch. Affected dogs may also point their nose into the air in order to breathe better. Sodium restriction (see page

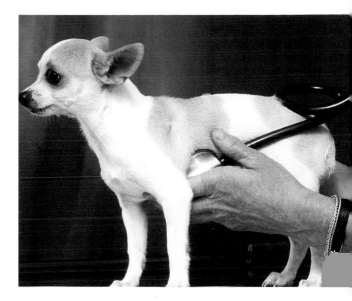

68) and several medications can make your dog more comfortable.

Tracheal Collapse is a problem to which Chihuahuas are much more prone than most other breeds. It is characterized by a dry, honking cough that occurs most often after exercise or when pressure is applied to the throat. See the sidebar on page 90 for more technical information about this condition.

Urinary Tract Diseases

Urine should be yellow to amber in color and clear, not cloudy. If your Chihuahua has difficulty or pain when urinating, urinates suddenly and often but in small amounts, or passes cloudy or bloody urine, he may be suffering from a problem of the bladder, urethra, or prostate. Dribbling dogs. The earliest symptom is usually increased urination. Although the excessive urination may cause problems in keeping your house clean or your night's sleep intact, never try to restrict water from a dog with kidney disease. Increased urination can also be a sign of diabetes or a urinary tract infection. Your veterinarian can discover the cause with some simple tests, and each of these conditions can be treated. Diet management is a major part of managing these problems (see page 68).

In males, infections of the prostate gland can lead to repeated urinary tract infections and sometimes painful defecation or blood and pus

of urine during sleep can indicate a hormonal problem and occurs most commonly in spayed females. Urinalysis and a rectal exam by your veterinarian are necessary to diagnose the exact nature of the problem. Bladder infections must be treated promptly to prevent the infection from reaching the kidneys.

Blockage of urine can result in death. Inability to urinate requires immediate emergency veterinary attention.

Kidney Disease, which ultimately leads to kidney failure, is one of the most common ailments of older

in the urine. Castration and long-term antibiotic therapy is usually required for improvement.

Endocrine Disorders

The endocrine system includes several glands that secrete hormones. These are chemicals that travel via the bloodstream to cells and tissues in the body and regulate the function of these cells and tissues. The most widespread hormone-related disorders in dogs are diabetes, hypothyroidism, and Cushing's syndrome. Hypothyroidism has the least-obvious symptoms. They may include weight gain, lethargy, and coat problems such as oiliness, dullness, symmetrical hair loss, and hair that is easily pulled out. The hallmark of diabetes is increased drinking and urination. Sometimes increased appetite with weight loss occur. Cushing's syndrome (hyperadrenocorticism) is seen mostly in older dogs. It is characterized by increased drinking and urination, potbellied appearance, symmetrical hair loss on the body, darkened skin, and susceptibility to infections. All of these conditions can be diagnosed with simple tests and can be treated with drugs by your veterinarian.

Ay, Chihuahua!
Hypothyroidism

Hypothyroidism is one of the most commonly diagnosed disorders in all purebred dogs. Although it is not a common problem of Chihuahuas, it does occur in them. The thyroid glands are located near the dog's Adam's apple (larynx) in the neck. They produce calcitonin, a hormone necessary for normal calcium metabolism, and thyroxine (T4), a hormone that regulates metabolism and is essential for the normal function of many of the body's organs and systems. In some dogs, the thyroid gland does not make enough hormones. This usually occurs because the thyroid gland degenerates from being attacked by the body's own immune system or for other unknown reasons.

A correct diagnosis entails relating clinical signs of the disease with laboratory test results indicative of impaired thyroid function. Clinical signs include hair loss on the flanks, tail, or behind the ears; darkened and thickened skin, sometimes with scaling or seborrhea; weight gain; lethargy; intolerance to cold; slowed heart rate; and infertility, among others.

The simplest test for hypothyroidism is a blood test for baseline serum T4 level. This test, however, is recommended only for identifying dogs with normal thyroid function. It should never be used as the final test to diagnose abnormal thyroid function. Dogs with T4 levels in the higher or even middle part of the normal range are probably not hypothyroid. Dogs with T4 levels in the lower part of the normal range may be in the early stages of hypothyroidism.

Dogs with T4 levels below the normal range are suspected of hypothyroidism. Keep in mind, though, that dogs that are sick, have recently undergone anesthesia, or are taking some drugs (including steroids, some nonsteroidal anti-inflammatories, and anticonvulsants) may have a misleadingly low T4 value. Thus, dogs with low T4 values should have additional testing.

More definitive tests for hypothyroidism include free T4 measured by equilibrium dialysis (fT4ed) and canine thyroid-stimulating hormone (cTSH) measurements. In the cTSH stimulation test, T4 levels are measured before and six hours after the dog is given thyroid-stimulating hormone (TSH). A dog with a normally functioning thyroid should respond with a much higher level of T4. These tests entail greater expense. In cases where financial factors play a role, some veterinarians instead begin the dog on thyroid supplementation, which is relatively inexpensive, and see if the symptoms resolve. The dog is then weaned from the supplementation. If symptoms return, the dog is diagnosed with probable hypothyroidism. The drawbacks of this approach are that in the meantime, the real reason for the dog's problems may be overlooked and some dogs are not candidates for supplementation.

Treatment for hypothyroidism is with daily medication, monitoring progress, and retesting in about two months. It is important to perform the tests about four to six hours after thyroid medication is given in order to measure the peak value.

Eye Problems

When reducing the size of dogs, not all organs can be reduced to the same scale. Some, such as the eyes, have limits beyond which breeders cannot further miniaturize them. This means that the eyes of a Chihuahua are larger in relation to the skull, and sometimes eye sockets, than are the eyes of larger breeds. This often causes the eye to be more prominent in small dogs. More prominent eyes are more susceptible to injuries and even proptosis (actually being dislodged from position in the eye socket). Despite this, the Chihuahua has surprisingly healthy eyes.

Tearing: Squinting or tearing can be due to an irritated cornea or foreign body. Examine under the lids, and flood the eye with saline solution or use a moist cotton swab to remove any debris. If no improvement is seen after a day, have your veterinarian take a look. For contact with eye irritants, flush the eye for five minutes with water or saline solution. For injuries, cover with clean gauze soaked in water or saline solution.

A watery discharge without squinting can be a symptom of allergies or a tear drainage problem. A clogged tear drainage duct can cause the tears to drain onto the face rather than drain normally through the nose. Your veterinarian can diagnose a drainage problem with a simple test.

Keratoconjunctivitis Sicca: KCS, or dry eye, is a potentially blinding condition that too often goes un-treated. Tears are vital for the health of the cornea (the clear outer layer of the eye). When tears are absent or reduced, the cornea dries out, becomes dull looking, and eventually may become inflamed, infected, ulcerated, and opaque. It is an uncomfortable condition, and the eye will often have mucus discharge. KCS occurs more commonly in older dogs. Your veterinarian can diagnose the condition with a simple test; treatment is with tear stimulants and artificial tear replacements. Because many cases are believed to result from an autoimmune response, in which the body destroys its own tear glands, the use of am immuno-suppressive medication is one of the primary treatments. Other treatments, including surgery, are available for severe cases. The earlier the condition is caught, the better the chances for successful treatment. Even so, most affected dogs will need lifelong treatment.

Proptosis: The comparatively large eye can be displaced from its socket, most often as a result of trauma to the head. This is obviously an emergency that requires immediate veterinary attention if there is to be any hope of saving the dog's vision. Sometimes the eye will slide back if you pull the lids wide apart. However, the more you handle the lids and eye, the more the area will swell and the more you risk further injuring the eye. If it does not work with the first try, cover the globe with a moist sponge and prevent your dog from pawing at his face. Get to the veterinarian at once. The dog may have to be sedated to replace the eye. Sometimes the eye is so injured that vision is never recovered. Occasionally, the eye itself must be removed. The faster treatment is obtained, the better the chance of recovery.

Cataracts: As your Chihuahua ages, the lens of the eye naturally becomes a little hazy. You will notice this as a slightly grayish appearance behind the pupils. However, if this occurs at a young age or if the lens looks white or opaque, ask your veterinarian to check your dog for cataracts. In cataracts, the lens becomes so opaque that light can no longer reach the retina. As in humans, the lens can be surgically removed and even replaced with an artificial lens.

Lameness

Lameness can occur because of injury or from hereditary skeletal problems. A veterinarian should examine any lameness that persists without significant improvement after three days of complete rest.

Therapies: Ice packs may help minimize swelling if applied immediately after an injury. The reduced tissue temperature lowers the metabolic rate and inhibits edema and the sensation of pain. Cold therapy can be helpful for up to a week following an injury.

Small Talk
Hypoplasia of Dens

The first and second vertebrae (called the atlas and axis bones, respectively) are two large bones of the spinal column situated immediately behind the skull at the top of the neck. Along the center line of the axis vertebra is a long projection of bone called the dens (also called the odontoid process). This projection fits into the middle of the atlas vertebra somewhat like a peg. It helps to secure the two vertebrae relative to one another and to prevent any substantial up and down movement between them. In some Chihuahuas, the dens fails to develop properly (a condition called hypoplasia), so the atlas and axis are not as tightly joined. This allows greater-than-normal up and down flexion between the two bones. This excessive flexion displaces the axis bone toward the top of the neck. Since the spinal cord runs in a small canal formed by these bones, when the axis is displaced, it can compress the spinal cord. Symptoms can range from pain to paralysis of varying degrees. Treatment is aimed at removing the pressure from the spinal cord by surgically removing parts of the atlas and axis bones and by then stabilizing the neck by wiring the two bones together. Don't worry. The dog is still able to move his head and neck. Obviously, the first week or so after surgery, the dog must be absolutely quiet. With surgical intervention, the prognosis is excellent.

Heat therapy can be beneficial to older injuries. Heat increases the metabolic rate of the tissue, relaxes muscle spasms, and can provide some pain relief. Moist heat applied for about 20 minutes is preferable, although care must be taken to avoid burning. Other types of heat therapy are available that penetrate more deeply through the tissues. However, because they also carry a greater risk of burning, they should be performed only by an experienced person.

Complete rest and total inactivity are the best initial home care for any lameness. Rest your dog well past the time he quits limping. Exercise therapy is equally as important, but exercise must be controlled. Leash walking and swimming are excellent low-impact exercises for recovering dogs.

In many injuries in which the limb must be rested, passive motion can be important in preventing muscle contraction and maintaining the health of the joint. All movements should be slow and well within the joint's normal range of motion. Massage therapy can be useful for loosening tendons and increasing circulation.

Many injuries are quite painful and may require drug therapy for pain relief. Orthopedic surgeries can be particularly painful and almost always warrant analgesics. Pain has a self-perpetuating aspect, which means that it is easier to prevent than to stop.

Ay, Chihuahua!
Patellar Luxation

The dog's knee, or stifle, is the joint connecting the femur (thigh) bone to the tibia and fibula (shin) bones. The knee joint also contains three smaller bones, including the patella (kneecap).

The patella's inner surface normally glides up and down within the trochlear groove of the femur as the knee flexes and contracts. It is also secured by the tendon of the quadriceps muscle as well as the surrounding joint capsule. In some dogs, the groove may be too shallow or the quadriceps may exert too much rotational pull, occasionally causing the patella to ride over the ridge of the trochlear groove when the knee is moving. When the patella is out of place (luxated), it usually cannot return to its normal position until the quadriceps muscle relaxes. Relaxing the quadriceps causes the leg to straighten at the knee, so the dog will often hop for a few steps with his leg held straight until the patella pops back into place. As the patella pops both in and out of place, the dog feels some pain as the patella passes over the ridge of the trochlear groove, so some dogs may yelp. Depending on the severity of the condition, the patella may or may not pop back into place on its own. Four grades of patellar luxation severity are described.

• Grade 1: The dog may occasionally skip, holding one hind leg forward for a step or two. The patella usually stays in place, however, unless it is manually shifted out of position. It returns to its correct position easily.
• Grade 2: The dog often holds the affected leg up when running or walking, and the patella may not slide back into position by itself. When the leg is manipulated, it has a grinding feeling.
• Grade 3: The patella is permanently out of position. Even when the patella is manually placed back into position, it does not stay long. The dog will sometimes use the affected leg.
• Grade 4: The patella is always out of position and cannot be replaced manually. The dog never puts his weight on the leg.

Patellar luxation can occur in one (unilaterally) or both (bilaterally) hind legs. The patella can be displaced toward the inside (medially) or outside (laterally). In the Chihuahua, it is almost always displaced medially. A dog with bilateral, medially luxated patellas has a bow-legged appearance when standing. Medial luxation is usually present by four to six months of age, although the symptoms may go unnoticed for several years. It gets gradually worse with age because every time the patella pops out of position, it stretches the surrounding tissues that are needed to hold it in place. This can even wear down the edge of the trochlear groove. The abnormal wear can lead to arthritic changes, which are usually the most serious consequence of patellar luxation. An early evaluation of the severity of the condition can help prevent arthritis by allowing the owner to implement appropriate treatment in a timely manner.

If your Chihuahua has grade 1 or grade 2 luxation, you may be able to slow the progress by keeping the dog at a trim weight, building the muscles of the rear with steady, moderate exercise such as walking (especially up hills), and keeping the cartilage healthy with glucosamine supplements. Such a regimen may or may not prevent the condition from worsening. Surgery in which the soft tissue surrounding the patella is reconstructed is an option and may provide permanent relief if done in these early stages.

Grades 3 and 4 can be quite painful and cannot be treated with conservative measures. Surgery reconstructing both soft tissue and bone is needed to relieve these dogs' distress. In this procedure, any stretched tissues are tightened and sutured. If the groove is shallow or if one of its ridges is worn flat, the groove may have to be reconstructed. If the quadriceps muscle is pulling on the patella and causing it to luxate, the muscle may need to be realigned. Even after the surgery, the knee may not be operating at 100 percent, but it will be much improved. This improvement is much more likely if the veterinarian performing the surgery is experienced with this procedure.

Discuss with your veterinarian the pros and cons of various analgesics.

Hereditary Joint Problems: Disorders of the bones and joints are among the most common hereditary disorders in dogs. Fortunately, Chihuahuas are not subject to hip or elbow dysplasia, the bane of many large-breed dogs. However, Chihuahuas are subject to patellar luxation (also called luxated patella or slipped stifle, see page 100). This is a potentially debilitating condition common to many small dogs in which the kneecap slips out of position and causes the dog to hold his rear leg up for several steps at a time. Some Chihuahuas also suffer from neck problems that could be due to hypoplasia of dens.

Neural Disorders

The central nervous system is made up of the brain and spinal cord. Disorders of these structures, structures of the peripheral nervous system, or the chemicals (neurotransmitters) that influence them can result in degrees of impairment ranging from mild to deadly. In the Chihuahua, the major concerns that affect the nervous system are hypoglycemia (see page 127) and hydrocephalus. Chihuahuas, like dogs of any breed, can also suffer from seizure disorders.

Hydrocephalus: The brain contains several spaces, or ventricles, that are normally filled with cerebrospinal fluid (CSF). If there is an overproduction or slowed resorption of CSF, the ventricles become overfilled with fluid. This exerts pressure onto the brain and eventually damages it. This condition, called hydrocephalus, can be either primary (congenital) or secondary (caused by other factors). However, in Chihuahuas, it is usually primary. In fact, Chihuahuas have one of the highest incidences of primary hydrocephalus of any breed.

Many dogs with congenital hydrocephalus have a large, domed skull

Facial characteristics of hydrocephalus.

Additional diagnostic tests include radiographs, MRI, CT scans, and if an open fontanel is present, ultrasound. In most cases, hydrocephalus can be diagnosed by the time a pup is four months of age. More severely affected dogs may not survive that long, while moderately affected ones might have stunted growth. In most cases, hydrocephalus slowly worsens, but in some cases it stabilizes. In rare cases, it becomes abruptly worse. The latter is especially true if the dog undergoes a period of physical stress.

Treatment is difficult, and euthanasia is usually recommended in all but the mildest cases. Steroids and diuretics may be used to increase CSF resorption and decrease CSF production, respectively, but long-term use of these drugs can produce serious side effects. Surgical drainage by way of a shunt can have complications and requires the shunt to remain in place permanently. At this time, no good treatment option is available. However, you should always check with your veterinarian, or even a veterinary neurologist, for news of progress. Depending upon the severity of the particular case, many Chihuahuas have lived long lives with hydrocephalus. Even though they may have diminished intellectual abilities, they still know how to love.

Seizure Disorders: Seizures are not uncommon in dogs and may or may not have hereditary causes. Many environmental factors can contribute to seizures. The cause is often never determined. Epilepsy is usually diagnosed when a dog, especially a young

and an open fontanel, two traits that are also often seen in perfectly healthy Chihuahuas. Some veterinarians not familiar with Chihuahuas will see these features and erroneously diagnose hydrocephalus. Chihuahuas with domed skulls and open fontanels may or may not have hydrocephalus. More sophisticated tests or overt symptoms are needed before a diagnosis should be made. Other symptoms of hydrocephalus include seizures, slowed learning, incoordination, involuntary movements of the eyes, and visual problems. Many hydrocephalic Chihuahuas have widely set eyes that look toward the sides of the head so that a lot of the whites of the eyes show in their inner corners. This is referred to as setting sun sign or, more technically, bilateral divergent strabismus. Although the condition may be evident at birth, more often it is not suspected until the pup is several weeks, or even months, old.

dog, has repeated seizures for no apparent reason. Such dogs very likely have a hereditary form of epilepsy.

Seizures may be focal or generalized; the latter can be further subdivided into grand mal (convulsive) and petit mal (nonconvulsive). Generalized grand mal seizures are the type most commonly reported in dogs. They typically begin with the dog acting nervous and then exhibiting increasingly peculiar behaviors (such as trembling, unresponsiveness, staring into space, and salivating profusely). This preictal stage is followed by the ictal stage, in which the dog will typically stiffen, fall over, and paddle his legs and champ his jaws. The dog may also urinate, defecate, salivate, and vocalize. During this time, the dog should be protected from injuries caused by hitting furniture or falling down stairs (wrapping him in a blanket can help secure him) and from other dogs (dogs will often attack a convulsing dog). The ictal stage usually lasts only a couple of minutes. If it continues for more than ten minutes, the dog should be taken to an emergency clinic. After the ictal stage, the dog will remain disoriented, may be blind, and will pant and sleep. This postictal stage may last from minutes to days. A vet-

erinary exam of the dog, including a complete history and description of the seizure onset and activity, should be performed as soon as possible.

No specific tests are available to confirm a diagnosis of epilepsy, although some abnormalities in the chemical composition of cerebrospinal fluid have been identified in some epileptic dogs. Dogs with recurrent seizures can be treated with phenobarbitol, which is usually effective in preventing seizures. Another drug, potassium bromide, can also be prescribed if results are not satisfactory with phenobarbitol.

Because epilepsy occurs more often in some breeds than in others and often runs in families, it is believed to have a hereditary component. In the breeds in which it has been studied

Small Talk
Epilepsy

For more information about epilepsy, visit the Canine Epilepsy Resource Center at *http://www.rt66.com/~dalcrazy/Epil-K9.html*

most comprehensively, epilepsy appears to be inherited in a mode consistent with a single recessive allele (see page 111). Other evidence points to the probability that different genes cause epilepsy in different breeds, a situation that will delay the availability of a DNA test for it in all breeds.

Circulatory Disorders

The circulatory system can be thought of as two connected but separate circulations. The one we usually think of carries blood around the body. The one we seldom think of carries blood between the heart and lungs. This latter circulation is called the pulmonary circulation. Although not common, some Chihuahuas suffer from a possibly hereditary condition called pulmonic stenosis.

Pulmonic Stenosis: After blood is pumped through the body, the cells have used up much of the oxygen it contained. The blood returns to the right atrium of the heart and from there goes to the right ventricle. The pulmonary valve allows blood to flow from the right ventricle to the pulmonary artery, which takes the blood to the lungs where it is reoxygenated. In some Chihuahuas, the passage between the right ventricle and the pulmonary valve is abnormally narrow (the technical term is *stenotic*). This causes the heart to work harder to force the blood through. The heart compensates by essentially building up its muscles so that the heart wall of the right ventricle becomes thickened. For mild cases of stenosis, the heart is able to compensate effectively, and the dog will show no outward symptoms and need no treatment. Young dogs, even those with severe stenosis, rarely have symptoms because of the heart's compensation. However, middle-aged or older dogs may be easily tired when exercising, have shortness of breath, or even faint.

More severe stenosis may need treatment. Severity can be tentatively gauged by characteristics of the heart murmur, radiographs showing enlargement of the heart, and ultrasound of the heart (echocardiogram). However, a definitive description of the severity requires cardiac catheterization. This procedure, which measures the difference in pressure on either side of the valve, must be done under anesthesia. Balloon valvuloplasty is the best treatment for severe cases. A stiff balloon is inserted into a peripheral blood vessel and manipulated until the balloon is in the narrowed area of the heart, where it is then inflated to widen the passage. After stretching the passage, the balloon is deflated and removed. Balloon valvuloplasty restores normal heart function about 70 percent of the time. This procedure must be done by a veterinary cardiologist.

The previous information lists but a small sampling of the problems that can befall your Chihuahua. Special emphasis has been placed on problems to which Chihuahuas are more prone compared with most other breeds. For more comprehensive descriptions of disorders common to all breeds, the reader is urged to consult a veterinary care book.

First Aid

The time to prepare for an emergency is now, before you are too flustered to concentrate. Prepare a first-aid kit; place a photocopy of these or other first-aid instructions into it. Have your veterinarian's emergency phone number at hand. Follow the directions outlined under the specific emergencies, call ahead to the clinic, and then transport the dog to get professional attention.

Artificial Respiration

1. Open the mouth, clear the passage of secretions and foreign bodies, and pull the tongue forward.

2. Seal your mouth over the dog's nose and mouth. Blow gently into the dog's nose for two seconds, and then release. Remember that Chihuahuas have very small lungs, so do not blow too hard or too long.

3. If you do not see the chest expand, then blow harder, make a tighter seal around the lips, or check for an obstruction.

4. Repeat at a rate of one breath every four seconds, stopping every minute to monitor breathing and pulse.

5. If air collects in the stomach, push down just behind the rib cage every few minutes.

CPR

1. Place your fingertips from both hands, one on top of the other, on the left side of the chest about one inch (2.5 cm) up from and behind the point of the elbow.

Small Talk
When Good Dogs Eat
Bad Things
Dogs can eat a variety of strange and sometimes dangerous things. Small bones can become stuck across the roof of the mouth, causing the dog to claw frantically at his face. Sharp bone fragments and other foreign objects can pierce parts of the digestive tract. Some foreign objects, and even rawhide chews, can cause blockage of the intestines. Particularly dangerous are long, stretchy, objects, such as socks, that can pass into the intestines but then become lodged in the intestines as the intestines become bunched around them accordion style. Such situations may need emergency surgery.

2. Press down quickly and release.

3. Compress at a rate of about 100 times per minute.

4. After every 15 compressions, give two breaths through the nose. If you have a partner, the partner can give breaths every two or three compressions.

Seizures: A dog undergoing a seizure may drool, become stiff, or have uncontrollable muscle spasms. Wrap the dog securely in a blanket to prevent him from injuring himself on furniture or stairs. Remove other dogs from the area (they may attack the convulsing dog). Never put your hands (or anything) into a convulsing dog's mouth. Treat the dog for shock. Make note of all characteristics and sequences of seizure activity, which can help to diagnose the cause. See page 102 for more information about seizures.

Heatstroke: Early signs of heatstroke include rapid and loud breathing; abundant, thick saliva; bright red mucous membranes; and high rectal temperature. Later signs include unsteadiness, diarrhea, and coma.

Wet the dog down, and place him in front of a fan. If this is not possible, immerse the dog in cool water. *Do not plunge the dog into ice water;* the resulting constriction of peripheral blood vessels can make the situation worse. Offer small amounts of water for drinking.

You must lower your dog's body temperature quickly, but you do not want the temperature to go below 100°F (37.8°C). Stop cooling the dog when the rectal temperature reaches 103°F (39.0°C) because the temperature will continue to fall.

Even after the dog seems fully recovered, do not allow him to exert himself for at least three days following the incident. Hyperthermia can cause lasting effects that can result in death unless the dog recovers fully.

Hypothermia: Because of their small body size compared with body surface area, Chihuahuas lose body

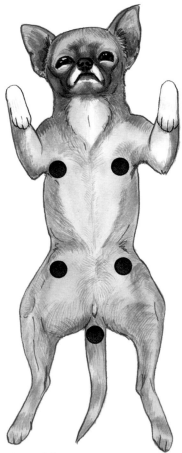

Pressure points.

heat at a faster rate than heavier dogs. This makes them more prone to chilling and hypothermia in cold weather. An excessively chilled dog will shiver and act sluggish. With continued chilling, the body temperature may fall below 95°F (35°C), the pulse and breathing rates may slow, and the dog may become comatose.

Warm the dog gradually by wrapping him in a blanket that has been warmed in the clothes dryer. Place plastic milk or soda bottles filled with hot water outside the blankets (not touching the dog). You can also place plastic over the blanket, making sure the dog's head is not covered. Monitor the temperature. Stop warming when the temperature reaches 101°F (38.3°C). Monitor for shock even after the temperature has returned to normal.

Hypoglycemia: Symptoms include drowsiness and incoordination. If the dog is awake, give him food, especially foods containing sugar. Add Karo (corn) syrup if you can get him to eat it. If the dog is unconscious, rub syrup onto his gums. For more information about hypoglycemia, see page 127.

Bleeding: Consider wounds to be an emergency if they bleed profusely, if they are extremely deep or large, or if they open to the chest cavity, abdominal cavity, or head.
• If possible, elevate the wound site, and apply a cold pack to it.
• Do not remove impaled objects; seek veterinary attention.
• Cover the wound with a clean dressing and apply pressure. Do not

Small Talk
The First-Aid Kit
• Rectal thermometer
• Scissors
• Tweezers
• Sterile gauze dressings
• Self-adhesive bandage (such as Vet-Wrap)
• Karo syrup
• Instant cold compress
• Antidiarrhea medication
• Ophthalmic ointment
• Soap
• Antiseptic skin ointment
• Hydrogen peroxide
• Clean sponge
• Pen light
• Syringe
• Towel
• First-aid instructions
• Veterinarian's and emergency clinic's phone numbers

remove blood-soaked bandages. Apply more dressings over them, and leave them even after bleeding stops.
• If the wound is on an extremity, apply pressure to the closest pressure point. For a front leg, press inside of the leg just above the elbow. For a rear leg, press inside of the thigh where the femoral artery crosses the thigh bone. For the tail, press the underside of the tail close to where it joins the body.
• Use a tourniquet only in life-threatening situations and only when all other attempts have failed.
• For abdominal wounds, place a warm, wet sterile dressing over any protruding internal organs, and cover with a bandage or towel. Do not

attempt to push organs back into the dog.

• For head wounds, apply gentle pressure to control bleeding. Monitor for loss of consciousness or shock, and treat accordingly.

• For animal bites, allow some bleeding, then clean the area thoroughly and apply antibiotic ointment. A course of oral antibiotics will probably be necessary. Not suturing most animal bites is best. However, a large one (over one-half inch [1.3 cm] in diameter) or one on the face or other prominent position may need to be sutured.

Limb Fractures: Chihuahuas have strong legs for their size, but their size nonetheless renders their legs susceptible to fractures. Lameness associated with extreme pain, swelling, or deformation of the affected leg, or grinding or popping sounds, could indicate a break or another serious problem. Attempts to immo-

bilize fractures with splints tend to do more harm than good. So keep the dog still, and cushion the limb from further trauma without splinting if you can get to the veterinarian right away.

Snakebite: Poisonous snakebites are characterized by swelling, discoloration, pain, fang marks, restlessness, nausea, and weakness. Most bites are to the head and are difficult to treat with first aid. The best first aid is to keep the dog quiet and take him to the veterinarian immediately. Antivenin is the treatment of choice.

Insect Stings and Allergic Reactions: Insects often sting dogs on the face or feet. Remove any visible stingers as quickly as possible by brushing them with a credit card or stiff paper; grasping a stinger often injects more venom into the dog. Administer a paste of baking soda and water to bee stings, and apply vinegar onto wasp stings. Clean the area and apply antibacterial ointment.

Call your veterinarian immediately if you think the dog may be having a severe reaction. Insect stings are the most common cause of extreme allergic reactions in dogs. Swelling around the nose and throat can block the airway. Other possible reactions include restlessness, vomiting, diarrhea, seizures, and collapse. If any of these symptoms occur, immediate veterinary attention will probably be necessary. Ask your veterinarian beforehand about keeping an antihistamine, such as liquid Benadryl, on hand for such emergencies.

Chapter Eight

Chihuahua Genetics and Breeding

Chihuahuas are among the most popular and beloved of all breeds, compelling many Chihuahua owners to try their hand at breeding a litter. Unfortunately, Chihuahuas are among the more difficult breeds for a novice breeder to work with, and Chihuahua breeding has many pitfalls.

Why Breeding Is a Bad Idea

You may have many reasons for wanting to breed your Chihuahua, but there are often many more reasons not to. The following are only a small sample.

Good Homes Are Hard to Find: The popularity of Chihuahuas may seem like one of the reasons in favor of breeding, but in fact it is not. More popular breeds actually have a more difficult time finding good, committed homes. Instead they attract an unusually large percentage of buyers who are acting on impulse, know nothing about the breed, and may be ill suited to own one. The Chihuahua's popularity has also attracted people to the breed who have the wrong intentions, many of whom mistakenly believe they can make money by selling puppies. The pup you unwittingly sell them may live his life as a puppy-making machine, only to be discarded when the entrepreneur discovers how poor a business venture Chihuahua breeding really is.

Costs: Fortunately, Chihuahuas have small litters, a fact that helps most of them find homes. This same fact makes Chihuahua breeding a

---

Small Talk
Tiny Chihuahuas
Tiny female Chihuahuas are precious companions—far too precious to risk their lives by breeding them. They are often too small to carry and whelp a litter without considerable danger to their health. They should never be bred without serious consultation with experienced breeders. Tiny males, on the other hand, can be bred to larger females in order to try to keep size down.

breed. They breed only the best specimens that have proven themselves in competition. They screen for hereditary defects in order to obtain superior puppies. Unless you have done the same, you are doing yourself, your dog, the puppies, any buyers, and the breed a great disservice. Remember the following.

• Unless your Chihuahua has proved himself by earning titles and awards or comes from an impeccable background, you may have a difficult time finding good buyers.

• Your Chihuahua should also have passed health clearances (see page 17).

• Breeding tiny dogs is not for novices. Risks to the dam and pups are much greater than risks in larger breeds.

• Selling puppies will not come close to reimbursing you for the health clearances, stud fee, prenatal care, whelping complications, caesarean section, supplemental feeding, puppy food, vaccinations, advertising, and staggering investment of time and energy.

losing proposition economically. Sales from an average litter of three pups will almost certainly not cover expenses and will certainly not cover your investment of time, energy, and worry. If you add a caesarean section—an all too common necessity to save the life of the mother and pups—you can see why Chihuahua breeding is a labor of love, not a money-making proposition.

First Do No Harm: Some Chihuahuas do find good homes, mostly with people who cared enough to do their homework and find good, responsible breeders. In other words, if you want to attract good homes, you need to be a good breeder. Responsible breeders have spent years researching genetics and the

The Perfect Match

If, despite all warnings, you are still contemplating breeding, be sure you breed the best dogs you can. It is assumed you've educated yourself

> **Small Wonder**
> Ch Quachitah Beau Chiene is the top-producing sire of American Champions, with 105 to this credit.

Small Talk
Mendelian Inheritance

Some traits are inherited in an all-or-none fashion. This Mendelian inheritance includes the familiar dominant versus recessive mode of inheritance. The dog has 39 pairs of chromosomes. Genes inherited from the sire and dam are located at the same locus (place) on each member of a chromosome pair. The same allele (alternate form of a gene) can be present on each chromosome at a particular locus. In contrast, at each locus, either of two or more alleles can be present. If both alleles must be identical in order for the trait they code for to be expressed, then they are termed recessive. If only one particular allele is needed in order for the trait it codes for to be expressed, it is termed dominant. Long versus smooth coats are a classic example of this type of inheritance. A long-coated Chihuahua must have two copies of the recessive allele that codes for long hair. A smooth-coated Chihuahua can have either two copies of the dominant smooth allele or one copy of each of the long and the smooth alleles. Many traits are not inherited in this all-or-none fashion. Such traits are called polygenic traits and depend on the interaction of many genes at different chromosomal locations.

The Stud Dog

A female worth breeding is worth breeding to the best male available. He should have earned titles and awards, which not only give an impartial evaluation of him but will also be helpful in finding good homes. Although no dog is perfect, you need to make sure the two dogs do not share the same faults. Family counts; the male should come from a consistently good background.

Health: The stud dog should have the same health clearances as your bitch and be in good general health. Both the male and female should be checked to ensure they are clear of canine brucellosis, a devastating communicable disease that can be sexually transmitted. An older (but still fertile) male is preferable, because he has already proved he can live to a healthy old age. If possible, you want to avoid using a very popular sire. Every dog has recessive deleterious

about your dog's strengths and weaknesses, have had the appropriate health clearances (page 17), and are familiar with Chihuahua lines and studs. It is also assumed you have a Chihuahua female that is not one of the teeny ones. Choosing a stud will involve several considerations.

Ay, Chihuahua!
Coat Color Genetics

Although color is immaterial to quality, it's human nature to prefer certain colors. The Chihuahua comes in one of the greatest assortment of colors of any breed. This makes predicting the coat color a little more complicated but a lot more fun!

The genetics of coat color inheritance have yet to be studied conclusively in Chihuahuas. To complicate matters, many colors can be difficult to describe accurately, especially in long-coated Chihuahuas. However, coat color inheritance is similar in most dogs of any breed, and it can be assumed that Chihuahuas share this hereditary pattern.

Coat color is determined by the interaction of several genes. When a locus has several alternative alleles, a dominance hierarchy exists. The distribution of white spotting in Chihuahuas provides a good illustration of a dominance hierarchy involving several different alleles at one locus.

White Distribution: Chihuahuas have four different alleles for different degrees of white spotting. Alleles for more white are always recessive to those for less white. In decreasing order of dominance, the alleles at the **S** locus are:

• **S:** Solid. These dogs have no white on them. A dog without any white must have at least one copy of the **S** allele. However, because **S** could mask the presence of any of the less-dominant alleles also at that locus, such dogs could be either **S/S**, **S/s^i**, **S/s^p**, or **S/s^w**.

• **s^i:** Irish-marked. Next in the dominance hierarchy is **s^i**, which causes the so-called Irish-marked pattern. The feet (and perhaps legs), tail tip, muzzle, and collar are white. Irish-marked dogs could have the genotype **s^i/s^i**, **s^i/s^p**, or **s^i/s^w**.

• **s^p:** Parti-colored. These dogs are predominantly white with patches of color. They can be either **s^p/s^p** or **s^p/s^w**.

• **s^w:** Extreme white spotted. These dogs are almost all white, with only small patches of color, most often around the ears or tail base. They have the genotype **s^w/s^w**.

The above is the traditional view of spotting inheritance, but it's recently been called into question by DNA studies that have only found one recessive allele responsible for partis, Irish-marked, and extreme white spotted dogs. In general, though, if you want a solid-colored puppy, at least one parent must be solid colored. You cannot get an **S** allele from spotted dogs, and you cannot get a solid dog without an **S** allele.

Color Distribution: Now that the white part of your Chihuahua is described, what about the parts with color? Think of a spotted dog as being splashed with white paint to varying degrees. The underlying color and pattern is genetically still there. For example, a tricolored dog (black, tan, and white) is simply a black-and-tan dog partially covered with a white muzzle and legs. The distribution of dark hairs is controlled by the interaction of genes at several different loci. Therefore, inheritance can, at times, seem very complicated.

One major locus is the **A** locus, which determines the distribution pattern of dark hairs. The Chihuahua has the following alleles at that locus:

• **a^y:** Sable. The **a^y** allele produces the tan or red coloration most often seen in the breed. These dogs are often born with a darker overlay that fades to a greater or lesser extent with maturity. The hairs may be mixed with darker hairs, somewhat like the color seen in Lassie-colored collies. A Chihuahua with Lassie's sable-and-white coloring would have alleles producing both the sable color at the **A** locus and the Irish-marked white pattern at the **S** locus. Sables can have the genotype **a^s/a^s**, **a^s/a^t**, or **a^s/a^d**.

• **a^t:** Tan point. The **a^t** allele produces dogs with a dark body coat and tan points above each eye, on the feet, and under the tail base, similar to the familiar pattern seen in Doberman Pinschers. Depending on genes at other locations, these dogs can be black and tan, chocolate and tan, or blue and tan. They can also have various amounts of white on them depending upon interactions with genes at the **S** locus. Tan point dogs can be **a^t/a^t** or **a^t/a^d**.

• **a^d:** Domino. The effect of the **a^d** allele is often hard to distinguish from that of the **a^y** allele. These dogs have a pattern in which dark hairs are tipped with black or brown and are lighter near the skin. They also have lighter legs, underside, and face, usually with a widow's peak or mask such as that seen in Siberian Huskies. They come in a variety of shades and colors. They may be combined with varying degrees of white spotting depending on interactions with the **S** locus. A domino Chihuahua can have only the genotype **a^d/a^d** at this locus.

The distribution of colored hairs determined by the **A** locus is complicated by interaction with alleles at the **E** locus. Its alleles have the following effects:

• **E:** Extension. This allows the formation of whatever pattern is determined at the **A** locus. These dogs can have the genotypes **E/E**, **E/e^{br}**, or **E/e**.

• **e:** Restriction. Dogs with two **e** alleles have no black hairs on their body, no matter what the alleles at the **A** locus dictate. Examples are cream Chihuahuas. These dogs must be **e/e**.

The distribution of black or brown hair is also influenced by genes at the **K** locus. It includes genes for dominant black and brindle.

• **K^B:** Allows for pure black (or brown dogs) without tan points. In dogs with **K^B**, the **E** locus then determines if the dog is black or red, and the **B** locus if he is black or chocolate.

• **K^{br}:** Produces dogs with dark, irregular vertical stripes running down the sides of the body over a lighter background. It is recessive to the dominant black allele.

• **K^y:** Allows for any patterns other than solid black or brindle. All black-and-tan dogs and all sable dogs are homozygous for **K^y**. You can't tell in reds and creams because of the masking action of genes at the **E** locus.

Besides the distribution of light and dark hairs determined by the alleles at the **S**, **A**, and **E** loci, the actual hue or color of the darker hairs is influenced by alleles at other loci.

The **B** locus determines whether dark hair will be black or chocolate.

• **B:** Black. The **B** allele allows black pigment to be black. Dogs with black pigment may be **B/B** or **B/b**.

• **b:** Chocolate. The **b** allele makes all black pigment appear brown. Dogs with **b/b** also have liver-colored noses and light-colored eyes.

The **D** locus acts in a similar manner as the **B** locus but determines if dark pigment will be black or gray.

- **D:** Dark. The **D** allele allows black pigment to be black. Dogs with black pigment may be **D/D** or **D/d**.
- **d:** Dilute. The **d** allele makes all black pigment appear gray. Dogs with **d/d** also have slightly lighter-colored noses and eyes.

Note, dogs with both **b/b** and **d/d** have a diluted tan gray color. This is appropriately termed *lilac.*

The **C** locus acts on red pigment.

- **C:** Full Color. The **C** allele allows for fully saturated reds. These dogs may be either **C/C** or **C/c**.
- **c:** Chinchilla. The **c** allele decreases the intensity of the red or tan pigmentation. Cream Chihuahuas could thus be **c/c.**

The **M** locus controls whether a dog is a merle or not. Merle refers to irregular blotches of dark color overlaid on a lighter shade of that same color, with both dark and light areas often interspersed with white hairs. It can be superimposed over other patterns, including tan points, in which case the points will usually be discernable. The extent varies so much that in some dogs, you have to really look before you find slight areas of merle. The pattern is caused by one copy of the dominant gene, **M**. One parent must be merle in order to produce a merle puppy.

What about two merle parents? That's a mistake. They can produce dogs with two copies of the **M** gene, which have a high risk of visual and hearing problems. Such dogs can often be identified becuase they have large areas of white on them. If you have a dog you suspect of being a hidden merle (one in which the merle pattern is hidden, often because the dog is a cream, red, or brindle), you must be careful not to breed him to a merle and accidentally produce double merle puppies. For this reason, not only shouldn't you breed a merle to a merle, but you shouldn't breed a merle to a cream, red, sable, or brindle, unless those offspring are neutered.

The foregoing is a basic description of Chihuahua coat color genetics. You can't predict everything, however, and every once in a while, a dog will be born that didn't seem to read the directions. Luckily, that's half the fun!

genes, even the nicest and most popular studs. Maintaining genetic diversity by breeding to an equally nice, but less-used, stud is far better for the health of the breed. Finally, in most cases, you should avoid breeding to a dog closely related to your bitch.

Size: Many people prefer a tiny male in order to produce small puppies. Keep in mind, though, that small size is only one of many considerations in producing Chihuahuas and is far from the most important one. Consider, also, that the tinier the puppies, the more difficulty you may have raising them to maturity.

Coat Length: The coat types may be crossed in the United States and Canada but not in all countries. The kennel clubs of several European countries, including the United Kingdom, will not register pups that result from a breeding crossing the two coat types. Be sure you understand the requirements of your kennel club before breeding.

The short coat is dominant to the long coat. This means that crossing two long coats will produce only long coats. However, a smooth coat may carry a recessive long-coat gene. Therefore, crossing two smooth coats may possibly produce both smooth and long coats. A long-coated Chihuahua with one or both parents that are smooth coats will have no less of a long coat than a dog from two long-coated parents. A smooth-coated Chihuahua resulting from a breeding of a smooth to a long coat will have no less of a short coat than a dog from two smooth-coated parents. Within each coat type, the relative length is determined by modifying genes that are inherited independently from the major smooth and long genes.

Relationship: If you see several names repeated in the proposed pedigree, you may wish to calculate how inbred the resulting puppies would be. The coefficient of inbreeding (COI) refers to the probability that a dog will have identical copies of the same gene that both trace back to the same ancestor. For example, the COI of pups from a sibling-to-sibling or parent-to-offspring mating is 25 percent. The COI from a mating of a half brother to half sister is 12.5 percent. You can calculate this by hand or with some computer pedigree programs.

Because many deleterious genes are recessive (meaning two identical copies are needed for them to exert their effects on the individual), avoiding breedings with high COIs is usually a good idea. As a general rule, dogs that are less closely related are more likely to produce healthy and long-lived offspring. Whereas dogs with high COIs are the results of inbreeding, low COIs result from outcrossing. Many geneticists now advocate breeding for the lowest possible COI. However, some compromises will likely need to be made in order to find a dog that otherwise fits your criteria.

Breeding and Whelping

Arrangements should be made with the stud owner well in advance of the breeding. A written contract should spell out what expenses you will be responsible for and what will happen if no puppies are born. The small litter size of Chihuahuas often makes it a bad idea to promise a stud fee puppy—you might not be left with one for yourself!

Estrus: Many Chihuahua females are fastidiously clean, and it's easy to miss when they first come into estrus. Count the days from the first sign of estrus carefully, but do not rely on them to determine the right day to breed. If you are shipping your bitch or if a lot is riding on this breeding, consider monitoring her estrous cycle by means of ovulation timing using blood samples. Vaginal smears can also give some guidance but are not nearly as reliable. An experienced stud dog is usually the most reliable indicator of the right time to breed, however. Most people breed the pair on alternate days for two to three breedings. Dogs ovulate all their eggs within 48 hours, so the idea that runts result from eggs fertilized from later breedings is not valid.

Gestation: Chihuahua gestation averages 61 to 63 days from the date of the first breeding, but full-term gestation can range from 57 to 72 days. This variability results from the fact that fertile matings can occur well before and after the actual time of ovulation. To get a better idea of the due date, you should use a progesterone test during the bitch's heat cycle. From this, your veterinarian can pinpoint the luteinizing hormone (LH) peak, which consistently occurs 64 to 66 days before whelping.

Pregnancy Determination: At around day 18 to 21, implantation occurs. During this time, some pregnant dogs will appear nauseous and even vomit. A canine pregnancy test (Reprochek) can detect the presence of relaxin, a substance produced by the placenta of a pregnant dog after implantation, typically by day 21 to 25 postfertilization. Human pregnancy tests do not work because, unlike in humans, even nonpregnant bitches have the same rise in the pregnancy hormones these tests detect as pregnant ones do. This is why dogs have pseudopregnancies. Normal dog physiology dictates that hormonally, pseudopregnant bitches are the same as bitches with real pregnancies.

Small Talk
Pyometra

Pyometra is a potentially fatal uterine infection that most commonly appears in the month or two after estrus. Symptoms may include a mucous discharge from the vagina along with lethargy and fever. Contact your veterinarian immediately if you suspect pyometra. If left untreated, it can be fatal. The best treatment is spaying, but medical drug therapy is sometimes successful for valuable breeding bitches.

By about day 35, pregnancy can be determined with ultrasound. Other signs that often develop by then are a mucous discharge from the vagina and enlarged, pinkish nipples. In the last week of pregnancy, radiographs can be used to count fetal skeletons. The knowledge of how many puppies to expect can be useful for knowing when the bitch has finished whelping.

Planned Caesarean Sections: One critical aspect of Chihuahua pregnancy is the size of the forming fetuses. Although newborn Chihuahuas are very small, they are not as small compared with their dam as are the fetuses of larger breeds of dogs. This means that a large litter often takes up so much room that the dam cannot carry it to full term. Even if she does, the chance of needing a caesarean section are greater since the pups seem to have difficulty aligning properly in the birth canal. On the other hand, a litter consisting of only one puppy can also be problematic since the pup may grow unusually large and cannot be whelped naturally. Having prior knowledge of the number and size of pups before the expected whelping date can help you decide with your veterinarian whether a planned caesarean might be the safest choice. This is also why using progesterone testing when breeding is a good idea.

It is the only way of pinpointing the exact day of ovulation and, from that, the exact due date. Although no one likes putting a tiny dog under anesthesia, statistics show that caesarean mortality rates are lower for planned caesareans than for natural births and certainly lower than those for unplanned caesareans.

General Care: The mother-to-be should be kept active throughout most of her pregnancy but should not be allowed to run and jump too vigorously as she nears her whelping date. She should begin to eat more, gradually switching to puppy food during the latter half of her pregnancy.

Whelping: Begin taking the expectant mother's temperature morning and evening every day starting about a week before the due date. When her temperature drops dramatically, to around 98°F (36.7°C) and stays there, you can anticipate pups within the next 12 hours. She will become increasingly restless and uncomfortable. Eventually, she will begin to strain with contractions.

The puppies are preceded by a water bag. Once this has burst, the first puppy should be born soon. If a puppy appears stuck, you can use a washcloth and gently pull it downward (between her hind legs) along with her contractions. Never pull a puppy by a limb, tail, or head, though. You may wish to help the mother clear the pup's face so it can breathe, and you may wish to tie off the umbilical cord. Do this by tying dental floss around the cord about 0.75 inches (1.9 cm) from the pup and then cutting the cord on the side away from the pup. Make sure that for every pup that comes out, a placenta comes out, too. Allow the dam to eat one placenta if she wants since they contain important hormones. However, they contribute to diarrhea, and one is enough.

Newborn Resuscitation: If a pup is born but is not breathing, do not lose hope. Remove any liquid from the mouth and nose by gentle wiping followed by suction with a bulb syringe. If the dog is not breathing,

**Small Talk
DNA**
A simple cheek swab can collect DNA for analysis in cases of pedigree disputes.

lessens the chance of being burned from hot surfaces. Continue to warm and stimulate the pup until he breathes on his own, cries, moves when stimulated, and has a heart rate of over 200 beats per minute.

If the pup still has no signs of life and you are ready to give up, do one last test. Drop the pup from a height of 6 inches (15 cm) onto a firm surface. Some pups with no detectable breathing or heartbeat will nonetheless subtly spread their limbs and pull them back quickly. These pups have sometimes been revived after even 30 minutes of stimulation and warming. Your veterinarian can better deal with a pup that needs help. If possible, the pup should get veterinary attention as soon as you can get him to the veterinarian without compromising warming.

you can carefully swing the puppy head first in a downward arc, supporting his head and body in a towel so it cannot slip out. Vigorously rub the puppy with a warm towel to stimulate breathing. Some breeders advise placing a finger dipped into brandy to the back of the tongue, which may cause the puppy to gasp. You do not want the pup to ingest alcohol, however, which is a depressant. Finally, you need to attend to the pup's circulation by placing him into moist, warm air. The best way to do this is by holding him over steaming water, taking care to keep your hand under him so you can detect if the heat is too intense. This raises the core temperature quickly and

Postnatal Care of the Dam

Not only must you be especially vigilant with Chihuahua puppies but with Chihuahua dams as well. A postwhelping exam is advisable to ensure that all pups and their placentas have been expelled. Sometimes a dead puppy is retained, causing a serious infection that often necessitates spaying.

Mastitis: You should check the dam's mammary glands throughout nursing for signs of mastitis, which include pain, bloody discharge, and both hardening and swelling. Home care includes hot compresses and gentle expression of the affected gland while preventing pups from nursing from that teat. Call your veterinarian for advice; antibiotics may be necessary.

Eclampsia: One of the greatest dangers to Chihuahua dams is the threat of eclampsia (puerperal tetany). It occurs when the amount of calcium lost in the milk is greater than the amount the body can absorb or produce. Eclampsia occurs most often during the first month of nursing but can also occur in late pregnancy. Small dogs, especially those with large litters that need a lot of milk, are predisposed.

Poor nutrition and improper supplementation can also contribute to the development of eclampsia. The optimal nutrition for the dam during the last half of her pregnancy and during nursing is a commercial puppy food. Because eclampsia occurs from too little calcium, many breeders try to avoid it by supplementing the dam with calcium during her pregnancy. However, this practice should be avoided because the excess calcium intake tends to decrease the body's efficiency in absorbing calcium from the diet and in mobilizing calcium from the bones—actually making eclampsia more likely. Supplementing with calcium during the first month of nursing, on the other hand, may be beneficial. You should discuss any supplementation with your veterinarian before implementing it, however.

Early signs of eclampsia include irritability, neglecting of pups, and restlessness, followed by salivation, facial itching, stiffness, fever, increased heart rate, and loss of balance. Final signs are severe muscle contractions and seizures. Eclampsia is a medical emergency that needs immediate treatment if the dam is to survive. Emergency treatment involves slow, intravenous administration of calcium. Following this, the pups should be weaned as quickly as possible.

Neonatal Care

Raising puppies of any breed is challenging. The work and worry they demand is incredible and is matched only by the entertainment and love

they provide. This is even more true with Chihuahua puppies. Neonatal puppies of any breed have a mortality rate of about 30 percent. In Chihuahuas, it can approach 50 percent, even with the best of care. Without the best of care, you can lose the entire litter.

Weight: You will need to weigh your pups on a gram scale daily. Although pups will likely experience a slight drop in weight the first day, after that they should steadily gain weight. The weight should double between days seven to ten. Most average-sized pups will gain around 4 to 7 grams a day during the first few weeks.

Cleft Palate: Monitor the puppies to make sure they are getting milk; pups with cleft palates will have milk bubbling out of their nostrils as they nurse. During normal development, the two sides of the roof of the mouth grow together and fuse before birth. In some pups, they fail to do so. This leaves an opening between the oral and nasal cavities, creating a number of problems. However, it can often be corrected surgically. Both genetic and environmental factors probably play a role. Prenatal administration of folic acid has been demonstrated to lower the incidence in some breeds.

Chilling: Puppies cannot regulate their body temperature, and chilling can kill them. Maintain the temperature in part of the whelping box at about 85°F (29.4°C) for the first week,

Small Talk
Vital Signs
Newborns should have a regular respiration rhythm, a heart rate of over 200 beats per minute, bright red gums, and a body temperature of 94°F to 96°F (34.4°C to 35.6°C).

80°F (26.7°C) for the second week, and 75°F (23.9°C) for the third and fourth weeks. Overheating and dehydration can also have just as devastating effects, so make sure the pups can crawl away from the heat.

Canine Herpes: Some neonates die for no apparent reason. Probably some of these are victims of canine herpes. Affected pups cry piteously and will not nurse. The herpes virus cannot replicate in high temperatures, and some pups have been saved by placing them into incubators at the first sign of symptoms. If you suspect canine herpes, keep your pups very warm, and consult your veterinarian immediately.

Hand Rearing

Abnormally small pups or pups that lose weight may need supplemental feedings. If the dam has eclampsia, mastitis, or is ignoring the pups, you will also probably need to supplement. Tube feeding newborn Chihuahuas is usually easier than bottle feeding, but you will need your veterinarian to show you exactly how to do this. If you have pups that will nurse from a bottle, you should use the bottle so that the pups' sucking instincts are satisfied. The pups should be fed every two hours for the first week or so of life, slacking off to every three hours once the pups have doubled their birth weights. The pups must be stimulated to urinate and defecate after each feeding. This is done by rubbing the urogenital area and anus with a warm damp cloth, simulating licking by the dam.

Small Talk
Hernias
Umbilical hernias, in which the opening around the umbilical cord fails to close properly, commonly occur in dogs. Most of them are small and eventually trap only a small pocket of fat. Larger hernias, or ones in which the abdominal contents can become trapped, should be corrected surgically. Although many people believe they come from the umbilical cord being pulled on during whelping, in most cases no such history exists. The hereditary aspects, if any, are not known.

Growing Up Chihuahua

If you plan to remove dewclaws, it should be done within the first three days. After that time, it is usually best to leave them on or wait until the pup is several months old and can be anesthetized for the procedure. Rear dewclaws should always be removed because they tend to be loosely attached and prone to injury. Some disagreement exists about whether also removing front dewclaws is best. However, many breeders feel doing so prevents painful injuries later in life.

Chihuahua pups are born with pink noses that gradually turn darker a few days after birth. The puppies' eyes will begin to open at around ten days of age and the ears at around two weeks. Around this time, they will also start attempting to walk. Be sure to give them solid footing—not slippery newspaper!

Weaning: Introduce the pups to pureed food when they are about three weeks old. Do this when they are hungry. You may have to put a bit onto their noses to get their tongues working and convince them this new substance is tasty. Some dogs catch on more quickly than others; don't worry if yours take a little longer. By about four to six weeks of age, the dam will begin weaning them herself, and the pups will start to prefer solid foods.

Socialization: Perhaps no other time is as exciting and rewarding in the life of a breeder than when the pups first venture out of the whelping

box and begin to explore the world. Your job now is to make sure that they are safe wherever they go and that they are gradually exposed to new experiences without being exposed to danger or disease.

You want your pups to meet new people when they are young. However, too often people carry with them communicable diseases that could kill your puppies. Do not indiscriminately allow visitors to handle your pups. Never allow anyone into your home who has come from a place where dogs have gathered, such as a dog show or animal shelter, unless they, at the very least, remove their shoes and refrain from handling the puppies. Although you may seem like less than the perfect host, your Chihuahua pups' lives are too precious and fragile to take any chances.

Although newborn pups do have some immunity they gained from their dam's first milk, this wears off at different times. You have no way to know just when you pups may be vulnerable. This is why vaccination is so critical for your pups' health.

Vaccinations

Vaccinations save lives. Without well-timed vaccinations your Chihuahua can be vulnerable to deadly communicable diseases. Your pup received his early immunity through his dam's colostrum during the first few days of nursing. As long as he still has that immunity, any vaccinations you give him won't be effective. But after several weeks that immunity begins to decrease. As his immunity falls, both the chance of a vaccination being effective and the chance of getting a communicable disease rise. The problem is that immunity diminishes at different times in different dogs. So starting at

Small Talk
Vaccine Adverse Reaction
Small dogs weighing less than 20 pounds (10 kilograms) seem to be at greater risk for having allergic reactions following some vaccinations; in fact, Chihuahuas are among the top five breeds most likely to have such a reaction. Affected dogs develop hive-like reactions, with raised, itchy whirls or swollen face or legs, within minutes to hours after a vaccination. Researchers believe they may be allergic to some component in the vaccine, and are comparing DNA from affected Chihuahuas with that of unaffected ones. To participate in the study, go to *www.vet.purdue. edu/k9vaxrxn*.

around six weeks of age, a series of vaccinations is given in order to catch the time when they will be effective while leaving as little unprotected time as possible. During this time of uncertainty it's best not to take your puppy around places where unvaccinated dogs may congregate. Some deadly viruses, such as parvovirus, can remain in the soil for six months after an infected dog has shed virus in his feces there.

Vaccinations are divided into core vaccines, which are advisable for all dogs, and noncore vaccines, which are advisable only for some dogs. Core vaccines are those for rabies, distemper, parvovirus, and hepatitis (using the CAV-2 vaccine, not the CAV-1, which can cause adverse reactions but is still sold by some feed stores). Noncore vac-

cines include those for leptospirosis, corona virus, tracheobronchitis, and Lyme disease. Your veterinarian can advise you if your dog's lifestyle and environment put him at risk for these diseases. Remember, more is not better!

A sample core vaccination protocol for puppies suggests giving a three-injection series at least three weeks apart, with each injection containing distemper, parvovirus, adenovirus 2 (CAV-2), and parainfluenza (CPIV). The series should not end before 12 weeks of age. A booster is given one year later, and then boosters are given every three years. Rabies should be given at 16 weeks of age, with boosters at one- to three-year intervals according to local law. Kennel cough and lep-

tospirosis vaccines must be given more often, once or twice a year, to remain effective.

Leptospirosis vaccine is the vaccination most likely to cause adverse reactions, especially in very young or very small dogs, and for that reason many veterinarians elect to omit it from the initial vaccinations. This is especially true if the dog does not walk in wooded areas or drink out of puddles where wild animals could have shed the bacteria.

Many owners of Chihuahua puppies object to the idea that their tiny puppies receive the same dosage of vaccine as do large-breed puppies, and some even split the dose in half. This is not good practice. The amount of vaccine has been calcu-

lated to elicit an immune reaction, and just as infection by a virus doesn't depend on how large the dog is, neither does immunity.

Deworming

Even pups from the most fastidious breeders can get worms. This is because some types of larval worms become encysted in the dam's body long before she ever became pregnant, perhaps when she herself was a pup. Here they lie dormant and immune from worming until hormonal changes caused by her pregnancy activate them. Then they infect her fetuses or her newborns through her milk.

Prevention: Internal parasites can be devastating for a tiny puppy. The number one prevention for most worms is daily removal of feces from the yard. Some heartworm preventives also prevent most types of intestinal worms (but not tapeworms). Over-the-counter dewormers are neither as effective nor as safe as those available from your veterinarian. Most deworming regimens require repeated doses several weeks apart to be effective. A stool check can determine the type of parasite your dog may have and direct the veterinarian to the best treatment for it. For these reasons, your Chihuahua should be dewormed only under the supervision of your veterinarian.

Roundworms: Roundworms (*Toxocara*) can be found in most pups. They can be spread to people as well as dogs by infested feces. Infected puppies can also become quite ill, with heavy infestations leading to convulsions or death. Symptoms include a rough coat, potbelly, and wasting muscles. Sometimes adult worms can be seen in vomit or feces. Puppies should be wormed at least twice for toxocariasis, and many protocols advocate more frequent worming.

Hookworms: Hookworms are especially prevalent in warm, humid climates. Puppies with heavy infestations have bloody, black, or tarry diarrhea and can become anemic and die. Adult dogs usually build up an immunity to hookworms, although some dogs have chronic hookworm disease.

**Small Talk
Heartworm**
Wherever mosquitoes are present, dogs should be on heartworm prevention. Monthly preventives do not stay in the dog's system for a month but, instead, act on a particular stage in the heartworm's development. Giving the drug each month prevents any heartworms from ever maturing. The most common way of checking for heartworms is to check the blood for circulating microfilariae (the immature form of heartworms), but this method may fail to detect the presence of adult heartworms in as many as 20 percent of all tested dogs. More accurate is an occult heartworm test, which detects antigens to heartworms in the blood. With either test, the presence of heartworms will not be detectable until nearly seven months after infection. Heartworms are treatable in their early stages, but the treatment is expensive and not without risks (although a less-risky treatment has recently become available).

Whipworms: Whipworms inhabit the large intestine. Heavy infestation can cause diarrhea, anemia, and weight loss. Unlike some other types of internal parasites, dogs do not develop an immunity to whipworms. Treatment consists of repeated deworming, often every other month for a year.

Protozoan Intestinal Parasites: Puppies and dogs also suffer from protozoan intestinal parasites, such as Coccidia and *Giardia*.

Coccidia are often associated with diarrhea, but many infected dogs show no apparent symptoms. Thus, the importance of Coccidia infection in dogs is not well understood at present. A stool sample is needed for diagnosis. Affected dogs respond well to supportive treatment and drugs to do away with the Coccidia.

Giardia is found fairly commonly in puppies and dogs. It can cause chronic or intermittent diarrhea but may also produce no symptoms. *Giardia* can be diagnosed with a stool sample and is more likely to be found in loose or light-colored stool. *Giardia* can be treated with drug therapy.

Hypoglycemia

Hypoglycemia is a disorder of the central nervous system that is caused by low blood sugar. It occurs most often in small, young, stressed or active dogs and is especially a problem of Chihuahua puppies. These dogs are not able to store enough readily available glucose. Therefore, once the available glycogen (the form in which the body stores glucose) is depleted, the body begins to break down energy stored in fat. However, small puppies have very little subcutaneous fat. When energy can no longer be derived from the liver or fat, the brain is deprived of its energy source and ceases to function properly.

Symptoms: Symptoms may appear suddenly and include sleepiness, weakness, and loss of appetite and coordination. If left untreated, the condition can worsen until the dog has seizures, loses consciousness, and dies.

Prevention: Small dogs that are ill, stressed, miss a meal, or are especially tiny or young are at greatest risk for hypoglycemia. A chilled dog, or a dog with parasites or diarrhea, is also more likely to become hypoglycemic. Some puppies are so active that they neglect to eat when they should. You can help to prevent a potentially life-threatening event by feeding your Chihuahua several small meals throughout the day. A puppy under the age of seven months should not go more than four hours without eating. Since this is seldom practical in the middle of the night, pups should be warm and confined at night so they do not expend a lot of energy playing and barking.

Meals should be fairly high in protein, fat, and complex carbohydrates (such as those found in starchy foods). Complex carbohydrates slow the breakdown of carbohydrates into sugars, which should lead to more efficient long-term utilization of sugars, and less overall fluctuation in blood glucose levels. Simple sugars (sucrose, sweets, and even semimoist foods, which have a high sugar content) cause the blood glucose level to fluctuate the most. This is because they stimulate insulin secretion, which can, in turn, cause the blood sugar level to drop in one-half to two hours. Thus, as a general rule, do not feed simple sugars to a Chihuahua, especially one predisposed to hypoglycemia. This rule has exceptions, however. If the dog is going to be exercising strenuously, you may wish to feed higher-sugar food immediately beforehand or during the exercise period in order to supply a quick source of added energy. In addition, a dog that is already showing signs of being hypoglycemic should be fed simple sugars immediately.

Treatment: If you suspect your dog is having a hypoglycemic episode, immediately feed him a high sugar content food. You can use corn syrup (Karo syrup is recommended) or even honey. If the dog cannot eat on his own, rub a bit of the syrup onto his gums and the roof of his mouth. Do not try to put the syrup or food down the dog's throat since the dog could choke on it. Keep the dog warm. You should see improvement within two minutes; use this time to call your veterinarian. Only after you have taken these first-aid measures should you rush to the veterinarian, where intravenous glucose treatment may be given. Once the

dog is stronger and able to swallow, immediately give him a small, high-protein meal (beef or chicken baby food is ideal at this time).

Hypoglycemia is mostly a problem of puppies (it may be related to immaturity of liver cells). Most Chihuahuas will outgrow it by the time they reach about seven months of age. All Chihuahua owners should be aware of the symptoms and treatments for the entire life of their dog, however, especially in times of stress.

The World Ahead

The puppies should get out to meet people and be socialized in the ways of the world. At the same time, you must be careful about exposing them to contagious diseases. Most reputable Chihuahua breeders prefer their puppies stay with them until they are at least 12 weeks of age, with tinier pups staying home even longer. Your pups should be leash trained and crate trained before they go to new homes. They should have spent time away from their litter-mates. They should have had some car-riding experience and met men, women, and children. During all this, they have probably burrowed deep into your heart.

If you can part with these babies without worrying about the situation you have chosen for them, you should not be breeding dogs. Good breeders worry. They worry that the people who seem to want a puppy so badly will change their mind in another year. They worry the people who seem so full of love may have

Small Talk
Saying "No"

How do you politely tell potential buyers that they cannot have one of your puppies? The first step is to screen carefully before you invite them to see the pups. Ask them about their previous pets, their intentions for their new Chihuahua, their living arrangements, and their family. Ask prying questions. If it is an older person, what would happen if the dog outlives the buyer? If it is a young couple, what would happen to the dog if they have a baby? If they are renting a home, what would happen if they had to move? No matter how hard you try, you may at times be faced with buyers who sounded fine over the phone but now that they are at your house, you see their children are wild or you just are not comfortable with them. Tell all potential buyers before they come that you never allow a pup to leave on the initial visit. Tell them it is your policy to have them go home and discuss the matter among themselves and that you, too, need to make some decisions. Then contact them, and tell them you've decided on another home or that you wish to keep the puppy. Of course, it is not easy—but it is part of the responsibility you undertook when you decided to breed Chihuahuas.

hidden explosive tempers. They worry that the description of the luxury accommodations is really a cage in the garage. Too many breeders have been burned by placing their faith in the people who seemed ideal, only to find out they were deceived. You need to listen with a cautious ear to what you are told, watch carefully how the entire family interacts with your dogs, and ask many, many questions. Your puppies are depending on you to weed out homes that could become living nightmares; they are depending on you for the rest of their lives.

When you finally find homes worthy of your pups, the hardest part of breeding a litter still awaits—saying good-bye to the pups you have grown to love. Of course, you could always keep them all.

Chapter Nine
Design of the Smallest Canine

Dog shows, and dog standards, have several purposes. In some breeds, the purpose is to predict how well a dog can perform the job he was bred to do from the way he's built. In theory, the dog that best meets the standard should also be the best-performing dog. In many of these breeds, the purpose of breeding is to improve the breed. In some other breeds, no pretense is made of evaluating for field performance. The Chihuahua is one such breed.

In these breeds, the purpose of breeding is often to preserve, rather than to improve, the breed. Dog breeds are living links to our past that must be recreated every generation. With each generation comes the possibility of creating a copy that is not as representative as the original. With additional generations of even less-representative copies, the original breed can be lost. Once lost, it is gone forever. The genes your Chihuahua carries are the same ones that may have witnessed ceremonial sacrifices and Spanish conquistadors. It is

the mission of the Chihuahua breeder to preserve a combination of the most representative genes in the healthiest Chihuahuas possible, to avoid forever losing a breed that is irreplaceable. The role of the breed standard is to provide a model to guide breeders in their choices for the next generation.

Breed standards are written by experienced breeders, often modeled after dogs they particularly admired. Understandably, many points of the standard are ultimately arrived at by compromise; a different group of breeders might arrive at a slightly different set of desirable features. This is why breed standards often differ slightly depending on which kennel club issues them. Despite this, most Chihuahua standards are in agreement about the major points of the breed. The standard drawn up by the Chihuahua Club of America and recognized by the American Kennel Club (AKC) is presented here; comments follow each section in italics. These comments are not part of the official standard and represent only one interpretation of it. After this information follows the standard recognized by the United Kennel Club (UKC).

The AKC Chihuahua Standard

General appearance: A graceful, alert, swift-moving little dog with saucy expression, compact, and with terrier-like qualities of temperament.

If you were limited to one phrase to describe the Chihuahua, this would be it. It conveys virtually everything you need to know to capture the essence of the breed. The rest of the standard supplies the finer—but still important—points.

Size, Proportion, Substance: Weight—A well balanced little dog not to exceed 6 pounds. **Proportion**—The body is off-square; hence, slightly longer when measured from point of shoulder to point of buttocks, than height at the withers. Somewhat shorter bodies are preferred in males. **Disqualifications**—Any dog over 6 pounds in weight.

Note that as long as the dog weighs 6 pounds (2.7 kg) or less, no preference should be given to one size over another. Both males and females are slightly longer than tall; this should be slightly more pronounced in females. This preference for longer bodies in females is seen in many breeds and reflects the belief that it gives the female more room to carry puppies.

Head: A well rounded "apple dome" skull, with or without molera. **Expression**—Saucy. **Eyes**—Full, but not protruding, balanced, set well apart—luminous dark or luminous ruby. (Light eyes in blond or white-colored dogs permissible.) **Ears**—Large, erect type ears, held more upright when alert, but flaring to the sides at a 45 degree angle when in repose, giving breadth between the ears. **Muzzle**—Moderately short, slightly pointed. Cheeks and jaws lean. **Nose**—Self-colored in blond types, or black. In moles, blue, and chocolates, they are self-colored. In blond types, pink nose permissible. **Bite**—Level or scissors. Overshot or undershot bite, or any distortion of

the bite or jaw, should be penalized as a serious fault. **Disqualification**— Broken down or cropped ears.

The Chihuahua's domed head is one of the hallmarks of the breed. The molera, or open fontanel (see page 18), is typical. Its presence or absence should not bear upon decisions of quality. The eyes should be large but set into the skull sufficiently deep so they are not bug eyed. The ears are set on the sides, rather than on top, of the head. When the dog is relaxed, they are carried so that they point to the ten o'clock and two o'clock positions. When the dog is alert, they are carried somewhat more erect, closer to the eleven o'clock and one o'clock positions.

A good Chihuahua head.

The muzzle comes off the skull abruptly at close to a 90-degree angle. A self-colored nose refers to nose leather that matches the coat color. In a level bite, the incisors (small front teeth) meet end to end. In a scissors bite, the front of the bottom incisors meet the rear of the top incisors. Other distortions might include a wry mouth (in which the bite may be overshot on one side and undershot on the other).

Neck, Topline, Body: Neck—Slightly arched, gracefully sloping into lean shoulder. **Topline**—Level. **Body**—Ribs rounded and well sprung (but not too much "barrel-shaped"). **Tail**—Moderately long, carried sickle either up or out, or in a loop over the back, with tip just touching the back. (Never tucked between legs.) **Disqualification**—Cropped tail, bobtail.

The neck has a slight arch, with the crest on top of the neck near the head, like a horse. A neck that is

Correct ear position.

arched in the other direction is called a ewe neck and is not desirable. The neck blends into the withers rather than joining it at an abrupt angle. The topline from the withers to the rump then continues on in a fairly straight line, neither going uphill nor downhill, and is neither swayed nor arched. The rib cage is not perfectly round but slightly ovoid vertically. The topline continues into the tail, which is set on fairly high at the level of the back. The tail is carried in a sickle shape, which means it curves upward midway as it approaches the tip. It can be carried either behind or up, even to the point of looping over and touching the back. However, it should not be carried down or tucked.

Forequarters: Shoulders—Lean, sloping into a slightly broadening sup-port above straight forelegs that set well under, giving a freeplay at the elbows. Shoulders should be well up, giving balance and soundness, sloping into a level back. (Never down or low.) This gives a chestiness, and strength of forequarters, yet not of the Bulldog chest. **Feet**—A small, dainty foot with toes well split up but not spread, pads cushioned. (Neither the hare nor the catfoot.) **Pasterns**—fine.

The forequarters carry most of the weight of the dog and must be strong even in a small dog. The forelegs should be straight when viewed from both the front and the sides. The combination of sloping shoulders and forelegs set well under the body is best accomplished by having a shoulder assembly and upper arm that join at an abrupt angle. This angle is often

Apple Dome Skull

Large Erect Ears

Tail Carried Up, Out, or Over Back

Short Slightly Pointed Muzzle

Dainty Feet

described as being 90 degrees since this is how it appears superficially. The elbows are close to, but not snug against, the rib cage. The feet are small. Cushioned pads mean the foot should be thick, not flat. The shape should be neither round nor long but in-between the two, a sort of rounded oval. The thickness of the pasterns often indicates the overall size of bone in the dog; fine pasterns call for fairly small bones.

Hindquarters: Muscular, with hocks well apart, neither out nor in, well let down, firm, and sturdy. The feet are as in front.

The hindquarters provide the propulsion for the dog and must be strong and well muscled. When viewed from the rear, they form a straight line of support to the ground. The hocks are short, so that the point of hock is close to the ground rather than high as in a horse.

Coat: In the **Smooth Coats,** the coat should be of soft texture, close and glossy. (Heavier coats with undercoats permissible.) Coat placed well over body with ruff on neck preferred, and more scanty on head and ears. Hair on tail preferred furry. In **Long Coats,** the coat should be of a soft texture, either flat or slightly curly, with undercoat preferred. **Ears**—Fringed. (Heavily fringed ears may be tipped slightly if due to the fringes and not to weak ear leather, never down.) **Tail**—full and long (as a plume). Feathering on feet and legs, pants on hind legs and large ruff on neck desired and preferred. **Disqual-ifications**—In Long Coats, too thin of coat that resembles bareness.

The coat on both coat types should be soft. A ruff (heavier coat around the neck and shoulders) is preferred. Having much of a ruff is difficult if the dog does not have an undercoat—which is not necessary on a Smooth Coat. The same is true for the longer hair under the tail. Long Coats should have wispy feathering on the ears and should not have a sculpted appearance.

Color: Any color—solid, marked, or splashed.

Any color, or combination of colors, is to be equally preferred.

Gait: The Chihuahua should move swiftly with a firm, sturdy action, with good reach in front equal to the drive from the rear. From the rear, the hocks remain parallel to each other, and the foot fall of the rear legs follows directly behind that of the forelegs. The legs, both front and rear, will tend to converge slightly toward a central line of gravity as speed increases. The side view shows good, strong drive in the rear and plenty of reach in the front, with head carried high. The topline should remain firm and the backline level as the dog moves.

When viewed from the side at a trot, the gait should be swift and sure. The front legs should reach forward a

good distance and the rear legs drive backward an equal distance. Hackney movement is not correct. When viewed from the front and rear, the legs move in a straight line of support from the dog to the ground. As the dog's speed increases, this line will converge slightly toward the center-line of gravity. However, the Chihua-hua does not single track (that is, reach a point at which the legs con-verge so much that all four feet fall onto the centerline).

Temperament: Alert, with terrier-like qualities.

The Chihuahua is no shrinking violet. It should be sure of itself and own the ground it stands on, almost to the point of being cocky.

Disqualifications:
• Any dog over 6 pounds (2.7 kg) in weight.
• Broken-down or cropped ears.
• Cropped tail, bobtail.

• In Long Coats, too thin coat that resembles bareness.

A dog that is disqualified cannot compete in conformation competition.

The UKC Chihuahua Standard

History: The history of the Chihuahua is lost in antiquity. It is known that both the Toltecs and the Aztecs kept dogs, some which were used for food, some for religious purposes, and some for companionship. Whether these dogs were Chihuahuas or not is uncertain. The breed came to the attention of the modern world in the mid-19th century when American visitors to Mexico brought the tiny dogs home. Chihuahuas first appeared in American dog shows in 1890. Today the Chihuahua is a popular companion dog. The Chihuahua was recognized by the United Kennel Club in 1948.

General Appearance: The Chihuahua is a small, active dog with a rounded skull; a short, pointed muzzle; erect ears that flare out somewhat to the side; and a sickle tail. The breed comes in all colors and color patterns and in both smooth and long coats.

Characteristics: Despite its small size, the Chihuahua is an alert, active dog with plenty of self-confidence. The Chihuahua's small size and devotion to its owner have made this breed a popular companion dog. Chihuahuas are courageous little watchdogs who are more than willing to defend their territory against strange people and dogs.

Head: The Chihuahua has a distinctive headpiece that is essential to correct breed type.

Skull—The skull is large and well rounded, sometimes called an "apple dome" or an "apple head." Viewed from the side, the line of the skull should curve in a semi-circle from the occiput around to the muzzle. The stop is vertical with the line of the skull, forming a 90-degree angle where it joins the muzzle. A molera may be present. Cheeks are clean.

Serious faults: Flat skull; stop with an angle greater than 90 degrees.

Muzzle—The muzzle is moderately short and somewhat pointed, although it should be broad and deep enough to support healthy dentition. Viewed from the side, the bridge of the muzzle forms a right angle to the line of the forehead. Lips are tight and clean.

Teeth—The Chihuahua has a complete set of evenly spaced, white teeth meeting in a scissors or level bite.

Serious fault: Overshot or undershot bite; wry mouth; crowded teeth; missing teeth; mouth unable to close.

Nose—Nose color varies with coat color. Accepted nose colors include black, brown, beige, pinkish-beige, or reddish-beige.

Eyes—Eyes are large and full but not protruding, and set well apart. Expression is bright and the eyes are luminous. Eye color varies with coat color, but dark eyes are preferred. Light eyes in dogs with pale coat colors are permissible but not desirable and may be brown, a light greenish or lemon-yellow, and ruby-red.

Ears—Ears are large, and erect, broad at the base and tapering toward their slightly rounded points. They are set so that the bottom edge of the ear is attached at the same level as the outer corner of the eye. The ears are normally carried so that the tips point slightly outward. This ear carriage is sometimes referred to as "at 10 o'clock and 2 o'clock," referring to the position of these numbers on a clock face. A line drawn from the outer corner of the eye to the inner corner and a line drawn from the inner corner of the eye to the tip of the ear form a 45-degree angle. When the dog is alert, the ears may be raised slightly. Long-haired Chihuahuas whose ears droop slightly as a result of the weight of heavy fringing on the ears are not to be penalized.

Disqualifications: Drop ears after six months of age; cropped ears.

Neck: The neck is of medium length and slightly arched, blending smoothly into well laid back shoulders. It is free from dewlap, and is thicker in males than in females.

Forequarters: Shoulders are clean and moderately muscled. There is good angulation between the shoulder blade and upper arm.

Forelegs—The legs are straight and of good length, with the elbows held close to the body. The pasterns are strong yet flexible. Dewclaws are generally removed.

Body: A properly proportioned Chihuahua is slightly longer (measured from prosternum to point of buttocks) than tall (measured from the withers to the ground), and length of the front leg (measured from point of elbow to the ground) should approximately equal one-half of the dog's height. Whether the dog is standing or moving, the line of the back is strong and level. The loin is moderately short and deep, with very little tuck-up. The ribs extend well back and are well sprung, but not barrel-shaped, forming a body that

would be heart-shaped if viewed in cross-section. The brisket extends to the elbow. Viewed from the side, the forechest extends in a slight, gentle curve in front of the forelegs.

Hindquarters: The hindquarters are muscular and the angulation of the hindquarters is in balance with the angulation of the forequarters.

Hind Legs—The legs are parallel to one another with good angulation at the stifle and the hock. Rear pasterns are short, well apart and vertical. Dewclaws should be removed.

Feet: Feet are small and oval-shaped with the toes well split up, but not spread out. Pads are well cushioned. Toenails may be any color.

Tail: The tail is moderately long, set on high, and never docked. It is thick at the base, tapering gradually to a point. Acceptable tail carriages include sickle or a single curl with the tip just touching the back. Tail carriage is an important characteristic of the breed. It should never be carried between the hind legs or curled below the backline.

Disqualifications: Cropped tail; bobtail.

Coat: The Chihuahua comes in two coat types, and it may be single- or double-coated. If undercoat is present, it is soft, dense, and close fitting.

Smooth Coat—The outer coat is soft, glossy, and close fitting. The hair is longer on the neck and tail. Sparse coat on the throat and abdomen is permitted, but hairless dogs are not acceptable.

Serious Fault: Bald patch.

Faults: Coat so short that hairs cannot be easily lifted; short hair on tail giving a rat-like appearance.

Long Coat—The outer coat is soft and fine, straight or slightly wavy. If undercoat is present, it should not be too thick. The coat forms feathering on ears, neck, back of legs, feet and tail.

Serious Fault: Long, billowing coat.

Color: Chihuahuas may be any color and may be solid colors, sable, brindle, or splashed with spots of color on a solid background.

Disqualification: Albinism.

Height and Weight: The ideal weight is between 3 and 6½ pounds, though smaller dogs are acceptable.

Disqualification: Over six pounds in weight.

Gait: When trotting, the gait is effortless, energetic, active and springy, with good reach and drive. The hind legs should move nearly parallel to each other so that the rear feet appear to land in the footprints of the front feet. At greater speed, there is a tendency to converge toward a center line of travel. The head is carried high and the backline remains firm and level.

Disqualifications: Unilateral or bilateral cryptorchid. Viciousness or extreme shyness. Drop ears after six months of age. Cropped ears. Cropped tail. Bobtail. Albinism. Over six pounds in weight.

So Your Chihuahua's Not Perfect

No dog—not even a Chihuahua— is perfect. The judge's job is to evaluate each dog's good points, decide what faults are the lesser evils, and try to rank all of the dogs in accordance with the standard. The breeder's job is similar. However, the breeder also factors in his or her knowledge of the dog's ancestry and health. The breeder also includes his or her own experience in determining which faults are easily bred away from and which virtues are most elusive. The owners' job is to evaluate their dogs objectively, admire them for their good points, forgive them for their shortcomings, and love them for themselves.

Chapter Ten
Little Show-Offs

Every Chihuahua owner knows that every Chihuahua is a champion in his own mind. Most owners are content with this self-proclaimed champion status, but others set out to prove it to the world. They enjoy the excitement that comes with showing off a beautiful and talented dog and with sharing the travels, trials, and tribulations that dog competitions provide. Although the best rewards of Chihuahua ownership are the intangible, everyday experiences, many people find that one way of memorializing the pride they feel for their partner is by earning awards and titles. You can share a perfect life with your Chihuahua without entering any competitions, earning any titles, or winning any ribbons—but it won't be nearly as exciting.

The Fairest of Them All

They strut about the ring as if the whole affair had been orchestrated for them. They don't hesitate to inform any other breeds they may compete against to get out of their ring—or else! They are the darlings of the show scene, the little dogs who would be kings or queens. It may look like a cuteness contest at first glance, but a dog show is far more than that. In conformation competition, each Chihuahua is compared with the Chihuahua standard, considering type, soundness, and temperament.

Show Training: What's the best way to get to Madison Square Garden? Practice, practice, practice. The Champion Chihuahuas that confidently trot around the ring at the Westminster Kennel Club Show in Madison Square Garden are the products of not only good genes and good luck but also of a lot of work. The judge has only a few minutes in which to evaluate each dog. A confident dog that struts his stuff will make a much stronger impression on a judge than one that tries to hide his attributes.

An upbeat attitude can make a Chihuahua really stand out from the crowd. A squeaky toy or liver is helpful in focusing the dog's attention and keeping him alert in the ring. Keep your Chihuahua happy so that he

doesn't let his tail drop while in the ring and so he comes to enjoy his time in the spotlight. The show Chihuahua must trot smartly beside you on lead and stand at attention in a show pose both on the floor and on an examination table.

Posing: In the show pose, the dog stands with legs parallel to each other and front legs and rear hocks perpendicular to the ground. The head and tail are held up, either naturally or by the handler. The dog must be able to hold this pose even when the judge goes over him, looking at his bite and feeling his body, ears, legs, and tail. During this individual exam, the dog is posed on an examination table. Usually, the handler will set each leg into place for this exam. At all other times, the dog will be posing when standing on the ground, so it is easier for the dog to pose himself (called free stacking). You teach your dog to free stack by training him with bait or a toy to stand attentively in a semblance of the show pose.

Begin by training your dog just as you would train him to do any other trick or exercise. Use a treat, and have him stand in front of you. Then say *"Pose,"* and give your dog the treat when he looks at the treat. Eventually, you will require your Chihuahua to look at the treat for a few seconds before getting it. Then you will require him to step forward a step or two until he is closer to a show pose. Usually that means first working on stepping forward with the front legs so that he is stretched out a bit rather than having his hind feet gathered under him. You can also use the treat to encourage your dog to stand with his feet parallel. Some dogs work better using a squeaky toy instead of bait. It's not uncommon for a dog—especially a Chihuahua—to lose interest in food or toys in the hubbub of a dog show, which is why socialization and training classes are important.

Gaiting: Posing is only half the fun. Dogs are also evaluated for how they move at a trot. Your Chihuahua should trot around with his head and tail up at a good, moderate pace (meaning you will be walking at a medium-to-slow walk). When the judge is looking at the dog's movement from directly head on or from the rear, you want your dog to be trotting in a dead straight line. To do this, you must be able to walk in a straight line, a feat surprisingly difficult when trying to keep one eye on your dog.

Practice: The biggest problem encountered in showing a Chihuahua is that even the bravest dog can be overwhelmed by the noise and activ-

Small Talk
Just the Facts
Contact the AKC for complete rules for AKC events or read them online at *http://www.akc.org/insideAKC/resources/rulereg.cfm*

ity of a dog show. Although your Chihuahua may be willing to take on one big dog, the sight of a hundred giant dogs and people may bring a cocky Chihuahua to his senses. This is not the case with all Chihuahuas. Much depends on how well your Chihuahua has been socialized to people, dogs, and noise.

Many outings will be needed before both you and your Chihuahua will give a polished performance. You can practice at informal matches meanwhile and, if you're lucky, join a handling class. You can hire professional handlers who will show your dog for you at AKC shows and probably win more often than you would. However, there's nothing like the thrill of winning when you're the one on the other end of the lead!

AKC Shows: AKC shows offer the following classes: Puppy (which may be divided into classes for 6 to 9 months and 9 to 12 months), 12 to 18 months, Novice, American Bred, Bred by Exhibitor, and Open. The Best of Variety class is only for dogs that are already Champions. All the male (dog) classes are judged before all the female (bitch) classes. Each class winner within a sex competes in the Winners class for points toward the championship title. The Chihuahua

Small Wonder
The top-winning Chihuahua of all time is Ch Holiday Gold Jubilee, who won 16 Best in Shows and 81 Toy group firsts. "Doc Holiday," as he was fondly known, was the first Chihuahua to be ranked the number one Toy dog in the United States. Having done everything ever asked of him, Doc was retired in his prime when only three years old.

that wins this class is called either Winners Dog or Winners Bitch, and wins up to 5 points, depending upon how many dogs he/she defeats. To become an AKC Champion (Ch), a dog must win 15 points including two majors (defeating enough dogs to win 3 to 5 points at a time).

Both the Winners Dog and Winners Bitch compete for Best of Variety against the champions. Only in specialty shows (special shows held by Chihuahua clubs) do the Long and Smooth Coat Best of Variety winners compete against each other for Best of Breed.

At the Show: Get to the show early so you can get a feel for what's going on and get your dog acclimated, but don't get him overheated or tired. Locate your ring, and watch the judge's pattern. Typically, the dogs in each class will enter in numerical order according to armbands (pick yours up from the ring steward about 15 minutes before Chihuahuas are to be judged). They will freestack while the judge checks them in and looks them over. Then the entire class will trot around the ring once. After that, the first dog in line is posed upon the exam table for the judge to inspect. Once the examination is finished, the judge will have the dog trot either directly away and back to him or her or in a triangle. Then the procedure will be repeated until the last dog has been examined. After that, all the dogs are posed or baited into position in line, and the judge may move them or switch them around or make some tentative

picks. If you are fortunate enough to win a ribbon, take it in stride. If not, take it in even better stride and congratulate the winner. One day that winner will be you.

Chihuahuas are only one of almost 150 breeds that may be at a dog show. Many of these larger dogs have never seen a tiny dog before and may not even realize your Chihuahua is a dog. Many of their owners are oblivious of the threat their dogs may pose. Never take chances. Carry your dog to ringside in a small carrier, and keep him there for his protection unless you are actively paying attention to your Chihuahua.

Do not make winning or losing the deciding factor as to whether you have a fun day at the show or not. Almost everyone who enters a dog show loses that day, because the

only dog that remains undefeated at the end of the show is the Best in Show winner. This means that you need to be able to separate your own ego and self-esteem from your dog. You cannot let your dog's ability to win in the ring cloud your perception of his true worth in his primary role: that of friend and companion. Because your Chihuahua is undoubtedly a real member of your family and the apple of your eye, having him placed last in his class can hurt. Just be sure that he doesn't catch on, and always treat him like a Best in Show winner whether he gets a blue ribbon or no ribbon at all. As long as you do that, you will always be a winner at the end of the show.

Junior Handling

The AKC offers Junior Showmanship classes for young people ages 10 to 18 years in which the person's ability to present the dog is judged rather than the dog's merit. Competitions for young people are a good way to instill confidence, poise, and good sportsmanship. They also give youngsters a goal and personal involvement in the day's activity. Perhaps one of these youngsters will grow up to become tomorrow's expert.

Small Wonder
The Best in Show record of 15 was held for an incredible 32 years by the great Ch Tejano Texas Kid until the current Best in Show record holder broke it in 1987.

The Chihuahua can be a good breed for a junior handler, especially a smaller handler who may not have the strength to control a large dog. A confident Chihuahua will almost show himself. Actually, one that shows himself off too well can make it look too easy and may make it somewhat difficult for the junior handler to show off his or her abilities!

Mind Games

Part of the pleasure of living with Chihuahuas is their keen ability to learn—which is not to say that they always do what you say! Combine this intelligence with the will to please you, and you have the makings of a spectacular obedience partner.

Rally: If your Chihuahua enjoys learning obedience, a good place to prove his mettle is in rally obedience, in which you and your dog go through a course consisting of 10 to 20 signs, each of which has instructions telling you which exercise to perform. Some of these exercises are moving exercises, such as heeling at various paces, turning, circling, stepping to one side, or calling your dog to you. Others are stationary exercises, such as having your dog lie down, stay, or pivot in heel position. You can talk to your dog throughout and repeat commands, but you can't pull him along on his leash or touch him. Points are deducted for mistakes, but a lot of leeway is allowed. The emphasis is on teamwork rather than precision. Each course is differ-

ent, and you won't get to see it until you arrive at the trial. That means you'll need to know all the possible exercises, even though you'll only be asked to do a subset of them. The Novice exercises are fairly simple, consisting of combinations of heeling, coming, sitting, and lying down.

More advanced classes include low jumps, 90- and 180-degree pivots to either direction (in which the dog stays in *heel* position at your side as you pivot, the dog starting and finishing in a *sit*), and an honor exercise, in which the dog remains in a *sit* or *down* position at the edge of the ring while another dog goes through the course. The honoring (staying) dog is on leash.

Each exercise has a particular sign with symbols that describe it, and

Small Talk
Therapy Dogs

Some Chihuahuas visit hospitals, nursing homes, and other situations where they can provide people with unconditional love, motivation to communicate, entertainment, or just somebody warm and cuddly to hug. Therapy dogs must be meticulously well mannered and well groomed and, above all, friendly and utterly trustworthy. You must do your part and protect your tiny therapist from patients who may not be able to control the force with which they hold or pet your Chihuahua. You must also be sure that no matter what, your dog will remain gentle and unperturbed. The Certified Therapy Dog letters are among the proudest a dog can attain.

each exercise has a particular way it should be performed. To find out more and see signs, go to *www.rallyobedience.com*.

Obedience Trials: In an obedience trial, each dog's performance of a set group of exercises is evaluated against a standard of perfection. The Chihuahua does not have a long history of selection for precision obedi-

ence. Only the exceptional Chihuahua will outperform a breed with centuries of selection based upon the ability to follow commands without question. That's what makes having that exceptional one such a thrill. It also provides a ready-made excuse for the times your dog's performance falls far short of exceptional. No matter how polished the performance, a Chihuahua in the obedience ring always attracts attention and admiration from onlookers. Spectators marvel that such a tiny dog can do his job in what is essentially a big dog's ring. Spectators also appreciate the times that the little dogs show off their ingenuity and sense of humor by creating their own set of rules!

A good obedience Chihuahua must be confident and outgoing. One of the most difficult exercises requires the dog to stand still while the judge examines him, touching the dog on the head and back. This can be extremely intimidating for any dog but especially for a small dog that sees a giant looming over him. A lot of socialization and practice are needed to convince your Chihuahua he should abandon what his good sense tells him to do and, instead, stand still as you tell him to.

You want your Chihuahua to be well trained and prepared before entering. You especially want your dog to be steady at the exercises requiring him to sit or lie down and stay with a group of other dogs for a required time. A small dog that gets up and runs away or that wanders over to another dog makes himself a

target for dogs that would otherwise be totally trustworthy. Don't tempt fate when something as important as your Chihuahua's safety is concerned.

Very small Chihuahuas are at a disadvantage compared with larger ones, because the distances and jump heights (8 inches [20.3 cm]) are the same. Tall grass can make some outdoor trials extremely difficult for tiny Chihuahuas.

AKC Competition Classes: The AKC offers successively more chal-

lenging levels of competition. *Novice* is the lowest level of AKC competition. To earn the Companion Dog (CD) title, a dog must qualify at three trials. Each qualifying score is called a leg. It requires passing each individual exercise and earning a total score of at least 170 points out of a possible 200 points. The *Novice* exercises include:

• Heel on lead, sitting automatically each time you stop, negotiating right, left, and about turns without guidance from you, and changing to a faster and slower pace.

• Heel in a figure eight around two people while still on lead.

• Stand still off lead 6 feet (1.8 m) away from you and allow a judge to touch the dog.

Small Wonder

Ch Bayard Believe It Or Not RJR is the top-winning Long Coat Chihuahua of all time, with 8 Best in Show wins to his credit.

• Do the same heeling exercises as before except off lead.

• Come to you when called from 20 feet (6.1 m) away and then return to *heel* position on command.

• Stay in a *sit* position with a group of other dogs, while you are 20 feet (6.1 m) away, for one minute.

• Stay in a *down* position with the same group while you are 20 feet (6.1 m) away, for three minutes.

Open is the intermediate level of AKC competition. To be awarded the Companion Dog Excellent (CDX) title, a dog must earn three legs performing these Open exercises:

• Heel off lead, including in a figure eight.

• Come when called from 20 feet (6.1 m) away but dropping to a *down* position when told to do so partway to you and then completing the *recall* when called again.

• Retrieve a thrown dumbbell when told to do so.

• Retrieve a thrown dumbbell, leaving and returning over a high jump.

• Jump over a broad jump when told to do so.

• Stay in a *sit* position with a group of dogs, when you are out of sight, for three minutes.

• Stay in a *down* position with a group of dogs, when you are out of sight, for five minutes.

Utility is the highest level of AKC competition. To earn the Utility Dog (UD) title, a dog must earn three legs performing these Utility exercises:

• *Heel, stay, sit, down,* and *come* in response to hand signals.

• Retrieve a leather article scented by the handler from among five other unscented articles.

• Retrieve a metal article scented by the handler from among five other unscented articles.

• Retrieve a glove designated by the handler from among three gloves placed in different locations.

• Stop and stand on command while heeling, and allow the judge to physically examine the dog with the handler standing 10 feet (3.0 m) away.

• Trot away from the handler for about 40 feet (12.2 m) until told to stop, at which point the dog should turn and sit until directed to jump one of two jumps (a solid or bar jump) and return to the handler.

• Repeat the previous exercise but jumping the opposite jump as before.

The Utility Dog Excellent (UDX) is awarded to a dog that earns ten legs in both Open and Utility classes at the same trials. This dog must have already earned its UD title.

The supreme AKC obedience title is the Obedience Trial Champion (OTCh). Unlike other obedience titles that require only performance to a standard proficiency, points toward the OTCh require performance of such precision that it is scored ahead of other passing dogs. A dog that places first or second in either Open or Utility classes earns a certain number of points depending on how many dogs were in competition. It takes 100 points, plus three first placements, to earn the OTCh. Understandably, very few dogs in any breed can claim such a prestigious title.

If you enter competition with your Chihuahua, keep in mind that in the years to come, the times you failed will bring you the best stories and the fondest memories. After all, passing is boring compared with the imaginative ways your Chihuahua can think of to fail! So be grateful for your passing scores, but don't forget to see the humor in your failing ones.

Agility

By jumping, climbing, weaving, balancing, and running through tun-

nels in a race against the clock, the littlest competitors in agility are changing a lot of spectators' ideas about just what these little Chihuahuas can do. Agility competition combines obedience, athleticism, and most of all, excitement. The AKC, United States Dog Agility Association (USDAA), and United Kennel Club (UKC) sponsor agility trials and award titles. Classes are divided by height, with Chihuahuas competing in the 8-inch (20.3 cm) jump height class for dogs 10 inches (25.4 cm) and under at the withers.

The obstacles are arranged in various configurations that vary from trial to trial. Handlers can give unlimited commands but cannot touch the obstacles or dog or use food, toys, whistles, or any training or guiding devices in the ring. Points are lost for refusing an obstacle, knocking down a jump, missing a contact zone, taking obstacles out of sequence, and exceeding the allotted time limit. To get a qualifying score, a dog must earn 85 out of a possible 100 points with no nonqualifying deductions. The obstacles and their requirements include the following.

• The A-Frame requires the dog to climb over two 8-foot-long (2.4 m long) or 9-foot-long (2.7 m long) boards, each 3 to 4 feet (0.9 to 1.2 m) wide, positioned so they form an A-frame with the peak about 5 to 5.5 feet (1.5 to 1.7 m) off the ground.

• The Dog Walk requires the dog to climb a sloping panel, walk across a suspended section, and walk down another sloping panel. Each panel is 1 foot (0.9 m) wide and either 8 or 12 feet (2.4 or 3.7 m) long. The horizontal bridge section is 3 or 4 feet (0.9 or 1.2 m) high.

• The Seesaw requires the dog to traverse the entire length of a 1-foot-wide (0.9 m wide) by 12-feet-long (3.7 m long) sloping panel supported near its center by a fulcrum base. So when the dog passes the center, the plank teeters to rest on its other end.

• The Pause Table requires the dog to stop and either sit or lie down for 5 seconds on top of a table approximately 3 feet square (0.3 m^2).

• The Open Tunnel requires the dog to run through a flexible tube. It is about 2 feet (0.6 m) in diameter, 10 to

20 feet (3.0 to 6.1 m) long, and curved so that the dog cannot see the exit from the entrance.

• The Closed Tunnel requires the dog to run through a lightweight fabric chute about 12 to 15 feet (3.7 to 4.6 m) long with a rigid entrance of about 2 feet (0.6 m) in diameter.

Small Wonder
The first Chihuahua to earn a UD title was Backman's Hot Chocolate, UD.

• The Weave Poles require the dog to weave from left to right through an entire series of 6 to 12 poles each spaced 20 to 24 inches (50 to 60 cm) apart.
• The Single Bar Jumps require the dog to jump over a high jump consisting of a narrow bar without knocking it off. **Note:** other single jumps are also permitted.
• The Panel Jump requires the dog to jump over a high jump consisting of a solid-appearing wall without displacing the top panel.
• The Double-Bar Jump (or Double Oxer) requires the dog to jump two 8-inch-high (20 cm high) parallel bars positioned 4 inches (10 cm) apart.
• The Triple-Bar Jump requires the dog to jump a series of three ascending bars in which the horizontal distance between adjacent bars is one-half the jump height and the vertical distance is one-quarter the jump height.
• The Tire Jump (or Circle Jump) requires the dog to jump through a circular object, approximately 2 feet (0.6 m) in diameter, resembling a tire suspended from a rectangular frame.
• The Window Jump requires the dog to jump through a 2-foot-square (0.2 m^2) window opening.
• The Broad Jump requires the dog to perform a single 16-inch (40 cm) broad jump over two boards.

Because safety is of utmost importance, all official jumps have

Small Wonder
Max (MACH2 Max NAC NJC) was the first Chi to earn the top AKC agility title of MACH—and he did it twice!

easily displaceable bars in case the dog fails to clear them. All climbing obstacles have contact zones painted near the bottom that the dog must touch rather than jumping off the top. All contact equipment surfaces are roughened for good traction in both dry and wet weather.

Training: Many obedience clubs are now sponsoring agility training, but you can start some of the fundamentals at home. Entice your dog to walk through a tunnel made of sheets draped over chairs. Guide him with treats to weave in and out of a series of poles made from several plumber's helpers placed in line. Make your dog comfortable walking on a wide raised board. Teach him to jump through a tire and over a hurdle. Teach your Chihuahua some basic obedience (*sit, down, come,* and *stay*). Make sure he's comfortable and under control around other dogs.

You need to condition your Chihuahua like any athlete to compete in agility. You also need to have a health check beforehand, making sure your dog is not lame, arthritic, or visually impaired. High jumping and vigorous weaving can impose stresses on immature bones, so these should be left until adulthood.

Small Wonder
Princess Terry-Jean, UDT was the first Chihuahua to earn a tracking title. UDT denotes she had both a UD and a TD title.

Chihuahuas Can Track!

One of the more mysterious, awe-inspiring, useful, and enjoyable canine abilities for which tests and titles are available is tracking—and even Chihuahuas can do it! Although Chihuahuas aren't the dog normally thought of as man-trailers, that's exactly what tracking Chihuahuas do. The way to start training your dog depends upon what motivates your dog. For chowhounds, you can begin by walking a simple path and dropping little treats along it. The dog will soon learn that he can find treats simply by following your trail. As training progresses, the treats get dropped farther and farther apart until, eventually, only the motherlode of treats is left at the end of the trail. Another way is to use yourself as the reward, requiring your Chihuahua to sniff you out from farther and farther away until he must follow your trail to jump into your arms.

Of course the actual tracking tests will require considerably more training than this. However, once you have taught your dog to follow his nose, you are on the right track!

AKC Tracking: The AKC offers several tracking titles:

The AKC Tracking Dog (TD) title is earned by following a 440- to 500-yard (402 to 457 m) track with three to five turns laid by a person from 30 minutes to 2 hours before.

The Tracking Dog Excellent (TDX) title is earned by following an older (three to five hours old) and longer (800- to 1,000-yard [732 to 914 m]) track with five to seven turns and with some more challenging circumstances. One of these circumstances is the existence of cross tracks laid by another track layer about one and one-half hours after the first track was laid. In addition, the actual track may cross various types of terrain and obstacles, including plowed land, woods, streams, bridges, and lightly traveled roads.

The Variable Surface Tracking (VST) title is earned by following a three- to five-hour-old track, 600 to 800 yards (549 to 732 m) long, over a variety of surfaces such as might be normally encountered when tracking in the real world. At least three different surface areas are included, of which at least one must include vegetation and at least two must be devoid of vegetation (for example, sand or concrete). Tracks may even go through buildings and may be crossed by animal, pedestrian, or vehicular traffic.

Competition provides a world of challenges and adventures for you to share with your Chihuahua. If you go only to win, you won't last long. If you go to have some fun and make some memories you'll cherish for a lifetime, the ribbons and titles will just be icing on the cake—and will actually come much more easily.

Chapter Eleven
Heart and Soul

Chihuahuas have a well-deserved reputation as being long-lived. Even so, they do eventually grow old. With good care and good luck, one day you will notice your perpetual puppy has finally calmed down. On closer inspection, you may realize his face has silvered and gait has stiffened. Many people have unrealistic expectations about life expectancy for their dog based upon the publicity given to unusually long-lived individuals. All dogs age at different rates. By 10 or 11 years of age, most Chihuahuas are showing some definite signs of old age. Even so, they continue to age slowly, and most Chihuahuas can live into their teens. Although the average life span is around 13 to 15 years, hearing of a Chihuahua living into his late teens is not uncommon. Occasionally, rare individuals even reach into their twenties.

However young at heart, at some point your Chihuahua will begin to feel the effects of age. You will need to know how best to help him cope.

The Best of Care

Even if your older Chihuahua refuses to act his age, some steps should be taken to ensure that he continues to feel young both in body and soul. That doesn't mean your dog has to go into retirement, however.

Behavior: While Chihuahuas of any age enjoy a warm, soft bed, it is an absolute necessity for an older Chi. Arthritis is a common cause of intermittent stiffness and lameness. It can be helped with heat, a soft bed, moderate exercise, and possibly

drug therapy. New arthritis medications have made a huge difference in the quality of life for many older dogs, but not every dog can use them. Ask you veterinarian to evaluate your dog. Keep your older Chihuahua relatively active, but do not put too much stress on his joints. If your dog is sore the next day, you have probably asked too much. Older dogs tend to like a simpler life. Lying in the sun, a short car trip, a tasty meal, a few laps around the house, a leisurely stroll around the block, and a chance to snuggle may be enough to make an older dog's day complete.

Boarding can be especially stressful for an older dog, but long trips can also be grueling. If you must leave your dog, consider getting somebody your dog already knows and accepts to house-sit while you are gone. Only the most responsible person should be entrusted with this task, however. The house sitter should be familiar with your dog and any health problems he may have. This person should be well versed in Chihuahua safety measures.

All Chihuahuas hate cold weather, and this is even truer for older Chihuahuas. They should wear a sweater if they go outside in the cold and be prevented from becoming chilled.

Your Chihuahua may not be able to jump onto or off of beds or chairs like he used to, either because of arthritis, general weakness, or visual problems. Try to arrange some steps or platforms that can help your dog reach the places he has enjoyed all his life.

Some older Chihuahuas become cranky and impatient, especially

familiar surroundings and extra safety precautions are followed. For example, block open stairways or pools, don't move furniture, and place sound or scent beacons throughout the house or yard to help the dog locate specific landmarks. Also lay pathways, such as gravel or block walkways outdoors and carpet runners indoors. Dogs with hearing loss can learn hand gestures and also respond to vibrations. It's never too late to teach an old dog new tricks.

Feeding: Keeping an older dog in ideal weight can be a difficult challenge. Both physical activity and metabolic rates decrease in older animals, so they require fewer calories to maintain the same weight. Excessive weight can place an added burden onto the heart and the joints. However, very old dogs often tend to lose weight, which can be equally bad. Your dog needs a little cushion of fat so that he has something to fall back on if he gets sick.

Most older dogs do not require a special diet unless they have a particular medical need for it (see page 68). High-quality (not quantity) protein is especially important for healthy, older dogs.

Older dogs should be fed several small meals instead of one large meal and should be fed on time. Moistening dry food or feeding canned food can help a dog with dental problems enjoy his meal. Dogs with arthritis, especially that affecting the neck, may find eating food that is elevated or eating while lying down to be more comfortable.

when dealing with puppies or boisterous children. Don't just excuse such behavioral changes, especially if sudden, as due simply to aging. They could be symptoms of pain or illness.

Sensory Loss: Older dogs may experience hearing or visual loss. The slight haziness that appears in the older dog's pupils is normal and has minimal effect upon vision. Some dogs, though, especially those with diabetes, may develop cataracts. These can be seen as almost white through the dog's pupils. The lens can be removed by a veterinary ophthalmologist if the cataract is severe.

Dogs with gradual vision loss can cope well as long as they are kept in

Arthritis: Joints occur at the moving junction of two bones. The ends of the bones are covered with cartilage, which helps to cushion impact and allows for smoother movement between the bones. The joint is enclosed by the joint capsule, the inner layer of which is the synovial membrane. The synovial membrane produces synovial fluid, a thick liquid that fills the joint cavity and provides lubrication and nourishment.

Older dogs often suffer from degenerative joint disease (DJD)—more commonly called arthritis. In some dogs, there is no obvious cause. In others, abnormal stresses or trauma to the joint can cause degeneration of the joint cartilage and underlying bone. The synovial membrane surrounding the joint becomes inflamed, and the bone develops small bony outgrowths called osteophytes. These changes cause the joint to stiffen, become painful, and have decreased range of motion.

Conservative treatment entails keeping the dog's weight down, attending to injuries, and maintaining a program of exercise. Low-impact exercise such as walking every other day is best for dogs with signs of arthritis. Newer drugs, such as carprofen, are available from your veterinarian and may help alleviate some of the symptoms of DJD. However, they should be used only with careful veterinary supervision. Some newer drugs and supplements may actually improve the joint. Polysulfated glycosaminoglycan increases the compressive resilience of cartilage. Glucosamine stimulates the synthesis of collagen and may help rejuvenate cartilage to some extent. Chondroitin sulfate helps to shield cartilage from destructive enzymes.

Senior Health

The older Chihuahua should have a checkup at least twice a year. Blood tests can detect early stages of treatable diseases. Although older dogs present a somewhat greater anesthesia risk, a complete medical work-up before administering anes-

Small Talk
Symptoms and Some of Their Possible Causes in Older Dogs
• Diarrhea: kidney or liver disease, pancreatitis
• Coughing: heart disease, tracheal collapse, lung cancer
• Difficulty eating: periodontal disease, oral tumors
• Decreased appetite: kidney, liver, or heart disease; pancreatitis; cancer
• Increased appetite: diabetes, Cushing's syndrome
• Weight loss: heart, liver, or kidney disease; diabetes; cancer
• Abdominal distention: heart or kidney disease, Cushing's syndrome, tumor
• Increased urination: diabetes, kidney or liver disease, cystitis, Cushing's syndrome
• Limping: arthritis, patellar luxation
• Nasal discharge: tumor, periodontal disease

thesia can be helpful in evaluating your dog's anesthesia risk.

The immune system may be less effective in older dogs, so shielding your dog from infectious disease, chilling, overheating, and any stressful conditions is increasingly important. At the same time, an older dog that is never exposed to other dogs may not need to be vaccinated as often or for as many diseases as a younger dog. This is an area of current controversy, and you should discuss this with your veterinarian.

Vomiting and diarrhea in an old dog can signal many different problems. Keep in mind that an older Chihuahua cannot tolerate the dehydration that results from continued vomiting or diarrhea, and you should never let these continue unchecked.

Like people, dogs lose skin moisture as they age. Though dogs don't have to worry about wrinkles, their skin can become dry and itchy. Regular brushing can help by stimulating oil production. Older dogs tend to have a stronger body odor, but don't just ignore increased odors. They could indicate specific problems, such as periodontal disease, impacted anal sacs, seborrhea, ear infections, or even kidney disease. In general, any ailment that an older dog has is magnified in severity compared with the same problems in a younger dog.

Periodontal disease is extremely common in older Chihuahuas, often the result of years of tooth neglect. The dog may lick his lips constantly, be reluctant to chew, or may even have swelling around the mouth. A thorough tooth cleaning, possibly with more extensive therapeutics, is necessary to relieve these dogs' discomfort.

Cushing's syndrome (hyperadrenocorticism) is seen mostly in older dogs. It is characterized by increased drinking and urination, potbellied appearance, symmetrical hair loss on the body, darkened skin, and susceptibility to infections. Diagnosis is with a blood test. Treatment is with drug therapy.

Dogs suffer from many of the same diseases of old age that humans do. Cancer accounts for almost half of all deaths in dogs over ten years of age. Some signs of cancer are abnormal swellings that don't go away or that continue to grow, loss of appetite or difficulty eating or swallowing, weight loss, persistent lameness, bleeding, or difficulty breathing, urinating, or defecating. Most of these symptoms could also be associated with other disorders. Only a veterinary examination can determine the real problem.

If you are lucky enough to have a Chihuahua senior, you still must accept that your time together is all the more precious and ultimately will end. Heart disease, kidney failure, and cancer eventually claim most of these seniors. Early detection can help delay their effects but, unfortunately, can seldom prevent them ultimately.

When You've Done Everything

Few breeds of dogs become such an intimate part of the family like Chihuahuas do. To many people, Chihuahuas really are their children—except they are perpetual babies always dependent upon their people. To others, Chihuahuas are true best friends, equal companions who share every part of the day. It's hard to believe that you will have to say good-bye to someone who has been such a companion, family member, and partner in adventure. Yet that time will come. Sometimes it seems like saying good-bye would be easier if they were just dogs—but they're not. Grief is the ultimate price that must be paid for love. It is a high price, but the years you have shared with your Chihuahua are truly priceless.

Grief: Denial is the first stage of grief and the first reaction dog owners usually have to the news that their dog has a terminal illness. It's a natural reaction that protects us from the emotional impact of the painful truth. It also goads many people into seeking a second opinion and exploring every possibility for curing their friend. Often, as it becomes clear that nothing can help, the next stage of grief is anger—anger that dogs live so short a time, anger that the treatments for humans are not available to dogs, and even anger at those who have older dogs. The third stage of grief is depression—when the truth is accepted and the futility of fighting acknowledged. Depression can begin well before actually losing a dog and last well after. It can involve such a feeling of helplessness and defeat that a person may not even try some reasonable therapies for his or her dog. Although depression is natural, protracted depression can be extremely damaging. As painful as grief is, it is hard to let go of, perhaps because to do so is finally to say good-bye. At that point, the last stage of grief is acceptance. Accepting the loss of a loved one doesn't mean you don't care. It just means that you realize that you have to do so in order to continue living and loving again. In deciding what is best for you and your dog and in getting through this terribly difficult part of your life, consider how your own stage of grieving may be affecting your decisions. Your veterinarian should be able to give you a more objective view of your options.

Euthanasia: Many terminal illnesses make your dog feel very ill. A point comes where your desire to keep your friend with you as long as possible may not be the kindest thing for either of you. If your dog consistently declines to eat, this is usually a sign that he does not feel well and a signal that you must begin to face the prospect of doing what is best for your beloved friend.

Euthanasia is a difficult and personal decision that no one wants to make. Consider if your dog has a reasonable chance of getting better and how your dog seems to feel. Ask yourself if your dog is getting pleasure out of life and if he enjoys most of his days. Financial considerations can be a factor if it means going into debt in exchange for having just a little while longer together. Your own emotional state must also be considered. For every person, the ultimate point is different. Most people probably put off doing something for longer than is really the kindest thing because they don't want to act in haste and be haunted by thoughts that just maybe it was a temporary setback. And of course, they put it off because they can't stand the thought.

We all wish that if our dog has to go, he would fall asleep and never wake up. This, unfortunately, seldom happens. Even when it does, you are left with the regret that you never got to say good-bye. The closest you can come to saying good-bye and then having your dog fall asleep forever is euthanasia. Euthanasia is painless and involves giving an overdose of an anesthetic. Essentially, the dog will fall asleep and die almost instantly. In a very sick dog, because the circulation may be compromised, this may take slightly longer, but the dog is not conscious.

If you do decide that euthanasia is the kindest farewell gesture for your beloved friend, discuss with your veterinarian beforehand what will happen. You may ask about giving your dog a tranquilizer beforehand or having the doctor meet you at home. Although it will not be easy, try to remain with your dog so that its last moments will be filled with your love. Try to recall the wonderful times you have shared and realize that however painful losing such a once-in-a-lifetime friend is, it is better than never having had such a partner at all.

Eternal in Your Heart

Partnership with a pet can be one of the closest and most stable relationships in many people's lives.

Many people who regarded their Chihuahua as a true friend and family member nonetheless feel embarrassed at the grief they feel at his loss. Unfortunately, the support from friends that comes with human loss is too often absent with pet loss. Some people who have never shared such a bond with a dog don't understand. Others who do may still not be able to express their feelings of condolences as readily as they would with human loss. Many people share and understand your feelings, however, and pet bereavement counselors are available at many veterinary schools.

After losing such a cherished friend, many people say they will never expose themselves to that kind of pain by loving another dog. Some

**Small Talk
In Loving Memory Gift**
One of the noblest tributes to a cherished Chihuahua is to donate in his or her memory to Chihuahua Rescue or to health research through the AKC Canine Health Foundation or the Chihuahua Club of America health fund.

also see giving their love to another dog as being unfaithful to the first. No dog will ever take the place of your departed dog, and the love you have for your friend will not be lessened by loving another. If you had so much to give and share with one dog, the only worse loss would be never sharing it again. Why not let a cold nose with a warm heart into your life and lap again?

Useful Addresses and Literature

Breed Clubs and Registries
American Kennel Club
www.akc.org

Chihuahua Club of America
www.chihuahuaclubofamerica.com

Health
Canine Health Foundation
www.akcchf.org

Morris Animal Foundation
www.morrisanimalfoundation.org

Orthopedic Foundation for Animals
www.offa.org

Rescue
Chihuahua Club of America
www.chihuahuaclubofamerica.com
(For a list of Chihuahua rescue
groups, click on "Breed Info.")

Chihuahua Rescue
www.chihuahuarescue.com

Chihuahua Rescue and Transport
www.chihuahua-rescue.com

Chihuahua Rescue USA
www.chihuahuarescueusa.org

Chihuahua–Toy Breed Rescue
and Retirement
www.crar.org

Petfinders
www.petfinders.com

Training
Association of Pet Dog Trainers
www.apdt.org

National Association of Dog
Obedience Instructors
www.nadoi.org

Periodicals
Chihuahua Connection
P.O. Box 579
Old Lyme, CT 06371
www.tazchi.com

Los Chihuahuas
12860 Thonotosassa Road
Dover, FL 33527

Top Notch Toys Magazine
8848 Beverly Hills
Lakeland, Fl 33809
www.dmcg.com

Web Pages
Big Chihuahua
www.bigchihuahua.com

The Chihuahua Page
*www.geocities.com/Heartland/
Plains/9231*

Club Chihuahua
www.clubchi.com

The Dog Agility Page
www.dogpatch.org/agility/

The Dog Obedience and Training
Page
www.dogpatch.org/obed/

Infodog Dog Show Site
www.infodog.com/main.htm

National Animal Poison Control
Center
(800) 548-2423
www.napcc.aspca.org/

Books
Coile, D. Caroline. *Encyclopedia of
Dog Breeds.* Hauppauge, New
York: Barron's Educational Series,
Inc., 1998.
____. *Show Me! A Dog-Showing
Primer.* Hauppauge, New York:
Barron's Educational Series, Inc.,
1997.

Index